DON'T LEAVE IT TO THE CHILDREN

STARTING, BUILDING AND SUSTAINING

A FAMILY BUSINESS

ALAN CROSBIE

DON'T LEAVE IT TO THE CHILDREN

First published in 2000 by
Marino Books, an imprint
of Mercier Press
16 Hume Street Dublin 2
Tel: (01) 661 5299; Fax: (01) 661 8583
E.mail: books@marino.ie

Trade enquiries to CMD Distribution
55A Spruce Avenue
Stillorgan Industrial Park
Blackrock County Dublin
Tel: (01) 294 2556; Fax: (01) 294 2564
E.mail: cmd@columba.ie

© Alan Crosbie 2000

ISBN 1 86023 115 2

10 9 8 7 6 5 4 3 2 1

A CIP record for this title is available
from the British Library

Cover design by Penhouse Design
Printed in Ireland by ColourBooks,
Baldoyle Industrial Estate, Dublin 13

CONTENTS

INTRODUCTION

HOW IMPORTANT ARE FAMILY BUSINESSES?

The short answer is: very important. At least 70 per cent of the companies in the world are family businesses, with the figure edging closer to 90 per cent in the East. They play a vital role in boosting the economy and in supporting employment.

Yet most family businesses do not survive past the first generation, and as few as one in ten lasts to the third. According to one academic who has done extensive study of the family-business phenomenon, family firms face a multitude of issues that other companies do not.

'In particular,' says Professor Ludo Van der Heyden of INSEAD in Fontainebleau, France, 'there is a mixing of family relationships involving emotional issues – often tacit rather than spoken – with hard managerial questions.'

That mixing of the emotional with the logical, the family with the managerial, can, on occasion, be lethal. The headlines, these last few years, have told of scandal, conflict, even murder within family businesses. Reports of such businesses have shown family members literally at each other's throats, in spite of being super-rich and enormously powerful. Intrigue and venom worthy of a medieval monarch's court have been demonstrated in rows that have made lawyers rich and cost workers their jobs.

I am part of one of the very few family businesses that

survive to the fifth generation. The Crosbies, who own and run Examiner Publications based in Cork, have hung togethere for a century and a half mainly through luck, male chauvinism and convenient death. When I took over as CEO, the paper was at a low point and looked to have a limited future. Now it is set to take on the other national newspapers in Ireland. Here again, luck and male chauvinism played their part – convenient death (touch wood) has not yet come into play.

But, in common with anybody who is involved with a family business, I am fascinated by the pressures and possibilities, the tensions and traumas, implicit in this kind of business. This book looks at some of the success stories – and a few of the tragedies – and seeks to identify the actions you need to take to ensure the success of a family business, whether you are a founder, a second-generation CEO, a fifth-generation shareholder or a non-family manager.

Alan Crosbie

1
—

THE CRAFTY OPPORTUNISTS

He scooped the journalists of Europe, my great-grandfather.
In a rowing boat.

Thomas Crosbie became a reporter at fifteen years of
age, in 1850. Not because he was seduced by the image of
the journalist as a pushy hack with a notebook in one
pocket and a packet of cigarettes in the other. It was a little
too early for that. Thomas Crosbie took to journalism
because there was neither a business nor a trade to inherit
from his father, who was a porter in a bank. So the son
went to work for John Francis Maguire, who in 1841 had
set up a newspaper called the *Cork Examiner*. It was a good
move, and Crosbie turned out to be a great reporter.

A dinghy was his way to reach the great ocean-going
liners as they pulled into Cork Harbour after their three-
week journey from the United States. Overshadowed by
the towering sides of the big ships, Crosbie would stand
up in the tiny boat, shout a welcome to the travellers on
their way to the port of London and follow up the welcome
with questions about what was in the news in America.
Sometimes, the people leaning over the rail would toss him
copies of *The New York Times* or another paper they had
picked up before embarkation.

The little boat rocking beneath him, he would flip the
pages of his notebook, filling them as quickly as he could

with the details shouted from above. He checked these details as he went, then thanked the travellers, swapped his notebook for the oars and made his way back to shore.

The *Cork Examiner*, thanks to his work, scooped the rest of Europe's press on various stories, including Abraham Lincoln's Gettysburg Address and the end of the American Civil War. The London *Times* did pretty well out of him too. Realising, early in his career, that his paper and the 'Thunderer' were not exactly in competition, he soon got into the habit of giving them second option on his stories. He would write his copy for the *Examiner*, then tap-tap-tap the information through to Fleet Street on the telegraph. Over time, the London editors noted that their long-distance 'stringer' not only captured stories they might otherwise not have, but that he wrote stylishly. Soundings were made. Would young Thomas Crosbie consider moving to London to become a full-time employee of the bigger newspaper? Thomas Crosbie indicated he would certainly consider it. Indeed, he would be happy to travel to Fleet Street to discuss the job offer.

The negotiations in London went well – up to the point where the employers-to-be copped on that their potential employee was a Catholic. Senior reporting staff in the London *Times* of the day were never drawn from the ranks of the Papists, and the offer of employment was politely withdrawn. (It is unlikely that Crosbie exacerbated the situation by announcing that his father had been born into a Protestant family but had converted to Catholicism to marry his mother.)

Thomas went back to Cork, where his first employer, John Francis Maguire, recognised his growing importance to the business by giving him more and more responsibility.

He eventually bought the paper in 1856 and it has stayed in Crosbie hands for five generations.

Today, at board meetings in *Examiner* headquarters in Academy Street, Cork, I now and again find myself looking at the portrait of Thomas Crosbie hanging to the left of the big window. I try – and always fail – to imagine the bearded, austere Victorian in the brownish painting as a romantic early hold-the-front-pager, beating Europe's media to stories of transatlantic assassinations, scandals and disasters.

One of the infuriating limitations of old paintings and photographs is how little they tell us of the personalities of the people they set out to portray. The same is true in many family businesses. The portrait of the founder is there – often, like that of Thomas Crosbie, in the place of honour in the boardroom – the eyes following the movements of the present generation; the expression serious, even reproving; the individual forever trapped in solid, male, middle-aged success, his expression telling no tales of enemies vanquished, obstacles overcome, setbacks sustained.

They can look peculiarly alike, the founders of great industrial dynasties, even though the reality is that their individuality far outweighs anything they have in common. But – certainly in the past – they did have some characteristics in common. One of the more obvious of these is that for most of industrial history, founders of family businesses tended to be male. As women could not be apprenticed, they could not learn crafts, and the early founders of businesses were usually craftsmen: the best in their business, whatever the business happened to be – and wherever the family originated. For example, in Italy, family business founder Salvatore Ferragamo was a wonderful shoemaker, while Guccio Gucci was a superb craftsman in leather.

Guccio Gucci was born in 1881, the son of a Florentine craftsman. He seems to have had dynastic notions, setting up the House of Gucci as a saddlery shop in 1906, but does not seem to have been totally committed, since, a few years later, he moved first to Paris and then to London, where he worked as a waiter in a prestigious hotel. Fourteen years of waitering intervened after he had first set up what seemed to be the beginning of a family business. Then he moved back to Italy to open the first Gucci shop, financed by the nest egg he brought back from London with him.

He was also sensitive to changes in the market. As his clients became more sophisticated, so did his offerings – his luxury luggage line in due course rivalling that of Vuitton. But he was to see neither the full exploitation of the Gucci brand nor the company's moves into overseas trading, dying as he did in the early fifties.

Salvatore Ferragamo was also a wonderful craftsman, known in his day as the Shoemaker of Dreams, supplying elegant footwear to Audrey Hepburn, Grace Kelly and Eva Peron. Again, although he was undoubtedly successful in his own terms, it was left to his widow to see and exploit the full, global potential of his name and products.

In other parts of Europe, family businesses grew out of trade rather than craftsmanship – and sometimes out of trade allied to prejudice. The great Jewish banking families of Europe carved out their niche largely because they were excluded, through prejudice, from involvement in myriad other activities. Another contributory issue was that money lending – 'usury' – was regarded as a taboo trade for

Christians. The confluence of these two factors helped great Jewish entrepreneurs build massive financial empires, while the very same prejudices, compounded by their success, exacerbated the Shylock stereotype created by envious Christians and most cruelly dramatised by Shakespeare in *The Merchant of Venice.*

One business founder who, although he belonged to a much later period than the centuries during which the Rothschild and other Jewish families were building their empires, nonetheless played his own part in propagating the worst racist myths against Judaism was the Irish-American Henry Ford. The man who was to create the world's biggest family business was born of two Irish emigrants. His father, William, had crossed the Atlantic in steerage in the decade of the Great Famine to join other members of his family, who had earlier left Cork, where they had been Protestant tenant farmers. His mother had been adopted by an Irish family which had come from Fair Lane (now known as Wolfe Tone Street) in Cork.

If we are to believe Henry Ford's later commentaries on his own life, it would appear that from a remarkably young age he was destined to be an inventor and entrepreneur. According to his self-generated legend, at seven years of age, having been shown the insides of a watch, he not only taught himself how to fix timepieces but would sneak out of the house at night to find broken watches belonging to neighbours in order to repair them. Along the same lines, the legend says that having, as a child, visited a file factory, he came home and not only made his own file but used it to turn his mother's knitting needles into corkscrews. (The legend does not, sadly, report his mother's reaction to this accomplishment.)

Henry Ford's legend of his childhood has much in common with that of other business founders. They tend – with some justification, it has to be said – to see themselves as rugged, fearless mould-breakers, talented beyond the average. Many of them also seem to need to believe that they overcame conditions of childhood poverty that make *Angela's Ashes* look comfortable.

Ford's siblings, for example, were less reverential than he was about memories of his technical tinkering as a toddler. 'When we had mechanical or "wind-up" toys given to us at Christmas,' one recalled, 'we always said, "Don't let Henry see them! He just takes them apart!"'

The siblings' memories diverged from that of their famous brother even more when it came to the deprivation he claimed characterised their childhood. That childhood, his sister later wrote, 'was neither as colourful and romantic as it has been painted, neither was it as full of hardship.'

This is an interesting distinction. The siblings who did not found a great business perceived their childhood to have been – well, *average*, even ordinary. The one who *did* found a great business perceived his childhood to have been extraordinary, particularly in the indications it gave of the genius for business he would later demonstrate. He also saw his childhood as having been damned beyond the ordinary by trials and tribulations. This, too, is significant, given that Ford's mother – who died when he was thirteen and who was, to the day her son died, a much-quoted influence on his thinking – had stressed the contribution hardship had made to human development.

'Life will give you many unpleasant tasks,' Ford remembered his mother telling him in the years before his teens. 'Your duty will be hard and disagreeable and painful to you at times, but you must do it. You may have pity on others, but you must not pity yourself.'

In one area of his later career, he undoubtedly lived up to this stoical creed. Almost a century before people with disabilities began to assert their right to equal treatment, Ford went out of his way to employ individuals who were handicapped in some way. The record also shows, however, that, despite his mother's warnings, he was not averse to self-pity, whether it was justified or not.

One of his claims to self-pity was that his father (as Henry saw it) did not have the vision to appreciate the significance of his son's mechanical bent and therefore did not foresee that, through the machines Henry created, he would change the world. Henry's portrayal of his less-loved parent emphasises the limited ambitions his father had for him – he wanted his son to grow up to be a farmer. The reality seems to have been that his father, who had quite a mechanical bent himself, did not stand in the way of his son's ambitions but rather supported him in his pursuit of them. The son's self-image may have required him to be seen to have overcome the unvisionary opposition of his father and to have followed the high standards of his mother.

The resolute way in which Henry Ford reinforced this perception of his own life had one important result: he went down in history as the indisputable founder of the family business. It is as if, like Topsy, he 'just growed' by himself and owed nothing to a line of succession.

In the nature of things, it is often quite difficult to identify the point at which a family business actually began – and even more difficult to separate what credit is due to a father and what to a son. As a result, it is probably no accident that many business founders work so hard, particularly in their later years, to create, edit and control their own myth. They want the 'Once upon a time' to start with them, rather than their parents. They see themselves as the beginners – the pioneers – even if their business was, in reality, based on inherited ideas or money. While they may, on occasion, be prepared to give some small credit to a mentor or parent, it is usually for a moral lesson; the business founder confirms their own value by living up to this moral lesson. They rarely give credit to previous generations for having passed on to them either money or a tradition of work, because to give such credit would be to confirm not their own value but the value of their forerunner. Business founders are frequently and unashamedly vainglorious in their self-portraits.

This sense of being special, different and gifted by God or fortune with a unique mission can lead to a self-centred and self-glorifying stance, such as that manifested by Henry Ford and by several of his fellow second-generation Irish-American entrepreneurs, notably the egregious Joseph Kennedy. Fortunately, however, it can also, on occasion, lead to a sense of moral responsibility which makes the founders much less eager to parade their own stories, much more willing to submerge their egos in order to achieve something they believe to be more important.

Two such founders were Bill Hewlett and David Packard of Hewlett-Packard. The two men met as undergraduates at Stanford University in the autumn of 1930 and, on graduation, decided to start a joint business, tossing a coin to work out which surname should go first in the title of their new corporation. In what became something of a tradition in high-tech start-ups, Hewlett-Packard's first workshop was a one-car garage in Palo Alto. Today, the corporation they created in that garage has more than 650 plants and offices in 120 countries throughout the world and is the only corporation in the Fortune 500 whose president is a woman.

As the two founders, after their marriages, tended to involve their wives in much of the strategic planning and values-development at Hewlett-Packard, the corporation fits one definition of a family business. Over time, what became the 'HP Way' developed. In effect, the HP Way means that Hewlett-Packard wants more than profits, revenue growth and a constant stream of new, happy customers – although all these are important. It also wants to stand for values such as diversity.

This commitment to diversity means that, in Ireland, although HP is a relatively young company – it set up in Leixlip only in 1995 – it nevertheless employs many workers who are in their late fifties and older. It also actively seeks to employ people with disabilities and men and women who have been among the long-term un-employed.

In his book about the company, David Packard remembers being taken aback during a conference he attended in the forties. At this conference, he expressed the view that employers had important responsibilities in relation to employees, customers, suppliers and the welfare of society at large.

'I was surprised and disappointed that most of the others disagreed with me. They felt their only responsibility was to generate profits for their shareholders,' Packard wrote later. 'Looking back, I suppose I shouldn't have been surprised. During the early decades of the twentieth century, profit was the businessman's sole objective. Labour was considered a commodity that could be bought and sold.'

Just how long approaches like the 'HP Way' are sustained in practice after the family business members who first developed them have moved away from active involvement is unclear. Some would suggest that what were passionately-held beliefs when the family members were centre stage can become little more than piously repeated shibboleths after these people are gone, although Hewlett-Packard seem, thus far, to have prevented that slide.

The two HP founders developed much – though not all – of the technology on which their empire was built, but there is also a tradition in the United States of great businesses being based on the inventions of some discoverer or innovator, although the innovators themselves did not always start the commercial dynasties. In fact, some of them demonstrated less than perfect commercial awareness of the application of their invention.

For example, when Thomas Alva Edison created the phonograph, he gave some thought to how it might be used, even publishing a newspaper feature proposing several ways in which he thought it might be useful. These proposed uses included teaching people how to spell and preserving the last words of dying people. Unsurprisingly, neither of these possibilities grabbed the public imagination, so, after a few years, Edison decided to market the machines for office dictation instead. Around the same time, other business people saw far more commercial possibilities in the same machine, creating and marketing the jukebox by rigging up the phonograph to play popular music at the drop of a coin. Edison took the dimmest of dim views of this, apparently seeing it as an insufficiently serious use of his invention.

On the other hand, Edwin Land and his wife not only built Polaroid out of Dr Edwin's invention of the instant camera but managed to be extremely swashbuckling about getting access to the facilities they needed to test out this bright idea. Before they were married, the two of them would go for a walk after dusk in an area where there was a well-equipped laboratory with a fire escape. Once they were sure nobody was in the area to see them, they would slip up the fire escape and let themselves into the laboratory to use the facilities for free until their need for sleep became overwhelming. Biographies of Land do not tell whether he retrospectively paid the owners of the lab for the time he spent working in it, developing his hugely successful invention.

Like Edwin Land, Werner Von Siemens used opportunities for research in fairly creative ways. Having joined the Prussian artillery at seventeen, largely to get training in engineering his family could not afford to give him, he made the mistake of acting as a second in a duel, which landed him in prison. Improving the shining hour while incarcerated, he carried out chemistry experiments that led, in 1842, to his invention of an electroplating process.

Siemens had the extra ability many business founders have of spotting potential in other people's inventions. When he saw an early model of the electric telegraph machine, for example, he instantly spotted its possibilities for international communication, and as he was already convinced that the business he planned would eventually be global – an ambitious vision, given that 'globalisation' as a corporate objective became generally fashionable only at the end of the twentieth century – he immediately began to try to improve it. Throughout his life, he was a technical problem-solver. He was the man who came up with the notion that gutta-percha could be used to insulate telegraph cables against moisture – a principle later applied to electric light and underwater cables.

He worked closely with his brother Carl to establish subsidiary factories in London, Vienna, Paris and St Petersberg. In this, he was somewhat out of the general run of founders, who frequently think in terms of the location where they started their business, rather than more globally.

Another exception to the local-is-best rule was Arthur Guinness, who in 1732 inherited £100 from the Archbishop of Cashel. He used that £100 – a vast sum of money at the time – to fund an experiment in a small brewery on the banks of the Liffey. By 1758, the experiment – stout-brewing – was a success. (Historians of brewing in Wales have recently claimed that what Guinness undertook was adaptation, rather than invention. They suggest that he first tasted dark ales in Wales and that stout was simply a variation on a product that had already been developed by the Welsh brewers.) One way or the other, when he knew, at the age of thirty-four, that he was on to a good thing, rather than expand locally, near Leixlip, Guinness decided the bigger premises he needed required him to move the business to St James's Gate in Dublin.

Each of the founders of famous family businesses seems to have had a personal skill, such as craftsmanship with leather; an innovator's instinct, such as the capacity to see beyond the first crude automobile engines to an industry based on mass production; or an inventor's genius, manifest in the ability to imagine what nobody had ever imagined before.

The one question they are unlikely ever to have asked themselves – and are never revealed by the records to have asked themselves – is, 'Will I start a family business?' Many of them knew they wanted to start a *business*, but the issue of family involvement was not a priority. It was either built into their thinking from the start or arose much later, as the business matured. According to the British Small Business Research Trust, the reasons people start businesses – family or non-family ones – have little to do with personal character traits.

'The frequency with which the self-employment option is chosen appears to depend greatly upon two key factors,' the trust says. 'First, the range or absence of alternative economic roles available to the individual. Thus, downturns in the labour market appear to result in upturns in the numbers of people becoming self-employed, and vice versa. Second is the availability of role models, particularly within the aspiring entrepreneur's own family.'

If your parents were self-employed, the law of averages gives you a better-than-average chance of becoming an entrepreneur, perhaps because you grow up understanding the risks and rewards of controlling your own industrial destiny. These days, if you have the instincts of an entrepreneur, you will find support systems available to you that were not available to earlier generations of business founders. For example, Dr Tony Ryan, the founder of Ryanair, is in the process of setting up a five-million-pound academy in west Dublin where entrepreneurs will learn about advanced technology and come to terms with business skills. The academy will be named after Ryan and funded by his three sons – a pleasing example of family solidarity.

DON'T LEAVE IT TO THE CHILDREN

Interestingly, however, the graduates coming out of the Dr Tony Ryan Academy for Entrepreneurship are much less likely than earlier generations to start specifically family businesses. This is because of a development noted in recent research commissioned by the accountants Grant Thornton.

'Businesses in high-tech areas are unlikely to become family-controlled,' says Andrew Godfrey of Grant Thornton. 'With the enormous growth of that end of the market, you will tend to see fewer family firms because of the basic desire to grow them and sell them. It's an inevitable shift.'

2
—

WHERE IN THE FAMILY?

In seeking for characteristics that are found in many of the legendary founders of family businesses, those who believe that birth order is a hugely influential factor in the way in which people's lives are shaped tend to credit the founders' successes to these people's positions in their original family. In this area, the most popular theory, advanced by Frank Sulloway in *Born to Rebel: Birth Order, Family Dynamics and Creative Lives*, is that first-born children tend to be supporters of the status quo, worshippers at the parental shrine and defenders of the family's values.

'This well-documented tendency is consistent with the general profile of first-borns as ambitious, conscientious and achievement-oriented,' writes Sulloway. 'Relative to their younger siblings, eldest children are also more conforming, conventional and defensive – attributes that are all negative features of openness to experience.'

Sulloway decided that one of the key points in history at which it was possible to contrast and compare rigid mindsets with flexible, open ones was the period when Charles Darwin published his *Origin of Species*. Sulloway, who examined the way in which people reacted to this seminal work in the immediate aftermath of its publication, maintains that his analysis of contemporary reaction divides unfailingly along the fault line of birth order: those who found Darwin's theory an outrageous attack on orthodoxy tended to be first-born, whereas those who were thrilled and excited by it tended to be later- or last-borns. While other scientists say they have failed to replicate his correlation, Sulloway's theory suggests that children who arrive later in the family sequence are more willing to take risks and are thus more likely to be found among business founders.

This is a theory more honoured in the breach than the observance, however. Henry Ford, for example, was not only not the youngest in his family, he was the second-eldest, although the eldest died at birth, thereby leaving young Henry as, in effect, Son Number One. P. T. Barnum, the great circus-master, was the first child of his father's second wife, the first wife having given birth to five children. Thomas Edison came smack in the middle of his family – he was the fifth-eldest of ten children. Looking at these family positions, it seems that the significant characteristics shared by family-business founders are something other than a place in the procession.

One characteristic founders of family businesses appear to share is intelligence. An obvious point? Perhaps. But it is an essential factor for any would-be entrepreneur to keep in mind. Just having the entrepreneurial urge and simply wanting to start a business (let alone a dynasty) is not enough. Usually, a high intelligence is needed too. The intelligence required by family-business founders is not always academic – not always measurable by how happy people are in school. Ben Cohen and Jerry Greenfield of Ben and Jerry's Ice Cream were not that happy or highly regarded at school, because both were chubby and unathletic. Ben had an exceptionally high IQ, balanced by an exceptionally low ability to apply himself to study. Jerry had a good memory and enough application to get himself into an advanced class in school. Both had messy, scattered college careers which left them with little but the idea that they'd like to go into business together, preferably selling some kind of food product.

A scattered or poor academic record is no great drawback to starting and building a successful business – Dell and Apple are two brand names that prove it – but a high IQ and a high level of curiosity tend to be associated with those who successfully start new businesses. At least as important, if not more so, than IQ is what is now being called the 'risk gene'.

In 1998, researchers at UCLA found that mutant genes play a role in causing personality traits that lead to increased risk-taking. The lead researcher, Dr Ernest Noble, said that 30 per cent of the population are born with one of the two relevant genes and that 20 per cent are born with both. Risk-taking and novelty-seeking – two of the characteristics associated with these genes – can, he pointed out, be a positive thing for inventors, entrepreneurs and explorers.

An interesting sidelight provided by this research is that having these genes means that one is more likely to parachute from planes, bungee-jump or become an alcoholic, smoker or drug abuser. This may in turn explain some of the behaviour associated with the second and third generation within many family businesses.

Most of the business founders I have mentioned thus far have been risk-takers in one way or another. While the physical appearance of my own great-grandfather, in the oil painting in the *Examiner* boardroom, gives no clue to him being either a risk-taker or a novelty-seeker, there are interesting clues, even in a relatively thin family history, pointing in that direction. His own father had abandoned his religion and his inheritance to marry a Catholic girl, ending up, as a result, in the humble role of porter in a bank. So the young reporter, standing up in the flimsy dinghy in Cork Harbour taking down the words of the Gettysburg Address, may have owed some of his gutsy inventiveness to his own father's mould-breaking genes.

The notion of entrepreneurs having possibly inherited a risk-taking instinct is supported by the family legends, which, again and again, tell stories of ancestors miraculously spared by disaster or magically enabled to survive hardship – stories which may well be the anecdotal illustration of a high-risk gene in play throughout the generations. A classic example of this is to be found in the story of the Binghams of Louisville, a dynasty associated with newspapers, which had its origins in County Down.

The Bingham family legend has it that the first arriving ancestor from Ireland got his initial directions to his new home in America wrong to the tune of 400 miles. Having arrived in the wrong place, and lacking a horse, he was going to have to trudge overland to where he should have been. Except, at precisely the same moment that this realisation dawned on him, he spotted on the path in front of him a diamond ring, which he then sold to buy transport to where he should have been in the first place. Later, as a Confederate officer, he was, by a combination of good luck and a capacity to improvise, to survive the Civil War and his consequent imprisonment as a prisoner of war. The qualities he showed at this time are demonstrated by him supplementing his prisoner's rations by eating mice he had managed to trap.

P. T. Barnum undoubtedly did not come by his risk-taking instincts by accident. His maternal grandfather was a notorious practical joker who had once managed to 'take' the entire crew of a ship on which he was sailing. The ship docked in one particular city on a Sunday, when all barbers were closed – but when plenty of other places, in which there were women to meet and impress, were open. Barnum, owner of the only razor on board, offered to shave every one of the crew.

The sailors were so delighted with his offer that they even went along with his idiosyncratic preference for shaving one side of each man's face first, then moving on to the next man, shaving one side of his face, and so on, with the promise that the second side would be tackled when all were shorn on side one. The only problem was that, when stropping the razor, as was necessary when he had so many individuals half-shaven, Barnum managed 'accidentally' to drop the blade overboard, leaving the crewmen with two choices: to stay aboard or go ashore in the certain knowledge that, half-bearded as they were, they would be ridiculed by all who encountered them. The grandfather of the man who created *The Greatest Show on Earth* was clearly prepared to go to considerable personal risk – such as by infuriating a ship-load of sailors – in order to get a laugh.

Marvin Zuckerman, the first psychologist to make an extensive study of what he calls the sensation-seeking trait, says that what is now being called the 'risk gene' comprises four elements:

- adventure-seeking
- experience-seeking
- boredom-avoidance
- disinhibition

People who score highly on a novelty-seeking table cannot stand repetitive tasks, routine experiences or bores. These are the people who never watch the same episode of *Fawlty Towers* again, no matter how funny it was the first time; who never read *The Bridges of Madison County* twice, even if they loved it the first time; and who get turned on by new ideas, new gadgets or new relationships.

'High novelty-seekers are better talkers and persuaders than listeners and order-takers,' points out molecular geneticist Dean Hamer in *Living with Our Genes*, 'which means they are better off starting their own businesses than joining large corporations.' This also means that those who voluntarily sign on with these people as spouses – and those who involuntarily sign on as offspring – often find themselves on a roller coaster that offers more in the way of punishment than reward.

In the nineteenth century, this factor was often concealed by the mores of the time. Thus, when we read that both of P. T. Barnum's wives had lengthy sojourns in sanitoria with 'nerves', we obediently summon up visions of Victorian women experiencing contemporarily correct 'vapours'. In fairness to these two women – and to many other spouses of early entrepreneurs – it must be suggested that their hospitalisations may, in retrospect, be more realistically interpreted as the only acceptable form of either protest or rebellion against their husband that was available to them.

If open rebellion against the obsessiveness of a business-founder-husband was not acceptable in the nineteenth century, it was hardly more acceptable in the early twentieth, as Rose Fitzgerald Kennedy, the matriarch of the Kennedy clan, found out. Her husband, Joseph Kennedy, not only involved himself in many businesses – not all of them strictly kosher – but was also a gross sensualist who had sexual affairs, including one with the silent-film star Gloria Swanson. Bizarre highlights of this affair included him running up the highest personal phone bill in the nation during 1929 when they were in different states and announcing to her on the day they were reunited that he had been faithful to her in the interim – his proof being that no other legitimate Kennedys had been conceived during that time.

Later researchers into the Kennedy family archive had to believe that Rose Kennedy was either a fool or a saint, given her unfailingly pleasant attitude to a woman who everybody else knew was her husband's mistress. Joe Kennedy was never a master of subtlety, and so brought his mistress into situations of close contact with his wife. Even up to a random encounter in the sixties, however, Rose Kennedy was sweet to Swanson. If she knew about her husband's affairs, she took payment for his infidelities in different – real – coin, travelling to Europe for months on end and patronising the best and most expensive designers in Paris and London. There is a view that when Kennedy Senior was later rendered speechless but cognisant by a major stroke, she effectively tortured him by making observations, in his hearing, that she knew would drive him to frothing distraction.

If the founders of family businesses have frequently been less than perfect husbands, they have even more often been lousy parents. Some of them simply travelled their way out of parental responsibility – a route greatly facilitated until relatively recently by the assumption that a woman's place was in the home, rearing the children, while the man was out being an innovator, pioneer or entrepreneur. Work-addiction is a nearly inevitable concomitant of business start-ups. People who work for owner/founders often complain bitterly about being telephoned in the middle of the night by their bosses, who assume that their business is the most important thing on everybody's agenda.

Workaholism on the part of a parent is brutally hard to bear for a child. Especially if, as often happens, it is presented by the parent as a virtue to be emulated. Many workaholics justify their absences from home on the basis that they are improving the standard of living of their wives and children. 'They give out to me for being away from home and they don't realise what they've got,' these workaholics say, pointing out that their family may have a better house, car or education than their peers. This, their argument goes, can only be sustained if the workaholic continues to stay at the office for incredibly long hours. The circular argument satisfies the workaholic but rarely makes sense to his or her family. The result can be distance between spouses and between the entrepreneur and their offspring, with resultant regrets later in the workaholic's life. It has been pointed out that no ageing business person has ever said that they wished they had spent more time in the office, but a great many have been heard to say they wish they had spent more time at home.

Not only do workaholics spend a great deal of time away from home, they also make such a virtue out of it that, by implication, they criticise those around them who lack their obsessive devotion to the job. The child who knows they don't have the virtue their father or mother possesses assumes that they should have and often experiences the lack as an inexplicable personal failure – a perception often repeatedly reinforced by the entrepreneurial parent.

Of all the famous founders of family businesses, Thomas Alva Edison may well have been the quintessential husband and father from hell. Edison rarely slept at home, and when he did, he not infrequently got into bed before taking off his shoes. Even remembering to wash was a chore for the inventor, whose lack of care for his appearance and personal life literally drove his first wife mad.

Edison seems to have regarded families as a desirable accessory but not as an essential. When his children – who were to live out their lives as clearly damaged human beings, starved of his love in their formative years – wrote to their mother from boarding school, he would take the letters and respond to them like a proof-reader, pointing out errors of grammar and spelling with ruthless cruelty while never expressing any affection for his offspring. When one of his sons exhibited the problems at school which might have been expected as a result of this treatment, the school authorities could not get Edison involved in any way in seeking a solution to the young man's problems. Mr Edison was far too busy to be bothered with such issues; they were to be referred to Mrs Edison instead.

So it was that, at sixteen, his son Thomas was writing that he felt so unhappy that he didn't know what to do. He had, he said, failed in everything he had tried. 'I don't believe I will ever be able to talk to you the way I would like to,' was the son's infinitely sad but realistic observation, 'because you are so far my superior in every way that when I am in your presence I am perfectly helpless.'

Edsel Ford, Henry Ford's son, had a better childhood, although ultimately his relationship with his father led to tragedy. Henry Ford was an indulgent father who loved gadgets and greatly enjoyed sharing them with his son. (Spending freely on their children seems to be a characteristic of business founders, perhaps to compensate for the amount of time they spend away from home.) He bought a camera before the turn of the century, and his early photographs have been described as full of 'clowning and goonery'. He taught Edsel (named after a lifelong school friend) to drive when the boy was only eight, and let him drive unaccompanied at that age.

On the face of it, this mutual regard continued when Edsel grew up and went into the business. The young man was much gentler and more self-effacing than his father, but there was never any doubt that he would be a key figure in his father's empire, although the 'great tribute' of naming a model after him turned out to be something of a back-handed compliment, since the Ford Edsel went down in automotive history as the all-time lemon.

At the heart of the affection between father and son, according to Ford biographer Robert Lacey, was a vacuum – the vacuum characterised by the inability to talk about really important things. 'Pride and rivalry, hope and disillusion – the love of Henry and Edsel Ford positively ached with contradictions, and as the two men failed to find ways to talk their conflicts out, the love grew less and the ache grew more,' writes Lacey.

Oscar Wilde, paradoxically, was the founder of a family business, in that one of his sons and his grandson ended up as writers and as conservators of the revived Wilde reputation. As a father, Wilde was remembered by his younger son as 'a smiling giant, always exquisitely dressed, who crawled about the nursery floor with us and lived in an aura of cigar smoke and eau de Cologne.' Wilde sang to his sons and made up stories for them.

The two boys were abruptly and permanently separated from their father after the scandal of his imprisonment. Their mother changed their surname after they were asked to leave a hotel room booked in the name of 'Wilde', and so the two boys grew up as Cyril and Vyvyan Holland. Cyril, who had been old enough to read newspaper posters at the time of the scandal involving his father, was haunted for the duration of his short life by his need to 'wipe that stain away' – a need which led him to the conviction that he must die an honourable death for his king and country. In 1915, Oscar Wilde's twenty-nine-year-old elder old son was killed by a German sniper on the battlefields of France.

Vyvyan, the younger son, came to terms with his father's past more equably, asking Robert Ross, a key figure in that past – and very probably one of Oscar's lovers – to serve as his best man when he married. Vyvyan actively participated in the restoration of his father's public reputation in the years that followed and never forgot the happiness of his childhood.

Read the biographies of the founders of family businesses, and one uncomfortable common feature jumps out at you: they are often willing, if not positively eager, to give credit for their successes to a parent, often a mother, who – they say – taught them discipline, duty, respect for others, or whatever is the set of virtues most likely to be claimed by each founder. They rarely if ever give credit to spouses or offspring. Henry Ford used to give high praise to his son Edsel when talking to journalists, but it was praise for Edsel as a nice guy and an able executive. Ford did not credit his son with influencing his own thinking – that honour belonged solely to his mother.

It would seem that there is something safe about giving credit to a parent, particularly a mother, but that giving credit to a friend, spouse or sibling might in some way detract from the kudos due to the central figure. As a result, each of these peripheral figures must be airbrushed out of the story – except in cases where including them will make the father figure feel better.

So Wendy's hamburger joints were named after their founder's daughter. This is a nice tribute to a nice kid, but it does not take any of the credit away from the hamburger man himself. Similarly, the Polaroid legend always mentions the fact that Dr Edwin Land's daughter asked, one Christmas after having had her photograph taken with the rest of the family, why she couldn't see the picture right then and there. Her clever father addressed himself very seriously to the innocent question, and out of his intellectual speculations and chemical experiments came virtually instant photography. Again, the story puts the child briefly centre stage, but only to get an even bigger round of applause for her father.

In some – admittedly fairly unusual – cases, founders or near-founders seem actively, if unconsciously, to set out to destroy the self-esteem of spouses and children and to confirm to them that they – the wife or child – have no possible contribution to make to the family business. One outstanding example of such an undervalued spouse is the case of Katharine Graham, who came to fame as the courageous owner of the *Washington Post* during the 'Deep Throat' Bob Woodward and Carl Bernstein revelations, which ultimately brought down President Richard Nixon.

Katharine Graham's father had owned the paper, and control of it had passed to her brilliant husband, Phil Graham, after their marriage. Although Katharine had been a competent journalist, Graham, after a time – and possibly as part of his developing a mental illness which ultimately drove him to suicide – set out systematically to rob her of any self-confidence she had. When she gained weight, he called her 'Porky' and gave her 'humorous' ornaments of fat pigs. He would exchange letters with her mother; these letters seemed to say, in effect, 'We two are so intelligent, and Katharine is so sweet but dumb.' At parties, if Katharine opened her mouth, he would fix her with a glance that silenced her.

'Yet, despite all this, I failed to recognise how aggressive his behaviour to me had become,' she was later to observe. 'I had learned so much from him that I felt like Trilby to his Svengali; I felt as though he had created me and that I was totally dependent on him.'

Why do so many different children of differently flawed parents end up in the family business? There are four possible explanations for this phenomenon:

- the roar of the rampant risk gene
- the wish of the powerful parent
- the confident ability of the younger family member
- the tragic dependence of the younger family member

Let me end this chapter with the fourth of these possible explanations. One of the most interesting and irreverent writers to examine why children turn out the way they do is Judith Rich Harris, who points to what she describes as the 'sad and paradoxical fact' that abuse may actually increase how clingy a child is. 'The abused child may go for comfort to the very person who abused her,' she writes, adding that this is true in other species too.

One wonders how many second- and third-generation individuals have gone into the family business not out of love of it but because a harsh childhood at the hands of the founder or key business figure left them incapable of making a living in any other field. A sad but important lesson from this for later generations is that most business founders have turned what they were good at, and what they enjoyed doing, into a career. Founders enjoy their business. Too many inheritors go into the business because they inherit it – but they don't enjoy it.

3

WHEN A FOUNDER ISN'T A FOUNDER

Although it is usually the founder of the business whose portrait hangs in the boardroom and figures at the beginning of the corporate history, the fact is that, not infrequently, it is the generation after the founder which expands the business beyond what is now called a 'lifestyle' operation, employing one or perhaps two other people.

In the case of Moffett Engineering of Clontibret, County Monaghan, the second generation, led by Carol Moffett, the daughter of the founder, changed beyond recognition what the first generation had done. Cecil Moffett bought a Ford Ferguson tractor for £250 at a spring show in 1940, in what his family saw as a gesture of faith in mechanisation as the future of farming. He quickly learned that, if he was going to get full value out of the tractor, it needed a range of implements and attachments, like ploughs, harrows and drills. The problem? The cost of these implements was way beyond his budget. The solution? He loved tinkering with bits of metal, so he set about designing and making his own implements. Within about five years, farmers in the surrounding area got to know about this and began to place orders with him for implements and metalwork.

The workshop was a shed at the rear of the family

farmhouse, and Cecil Moffett worked from dawn till dusk. Monaghan has a long tradition of furniture-making, mushroom-growing and poultry-processing. As time went on, Moffett's business changed direction. Whereas at the beginning his main customers had been farmers, he later found that he was making more and more customised pieces of equipment for the various industries in the area. Untrained in marketing, he instinctively tapped into the best kind of marketing there is: third-party marketing done by satisfied customers.

And then Moffett died suddenly. He left a small company, consisting of two employees and his son, Robert – who was sixteen at the time. The firm had no debt – but it had no great cash flow either.

'At the time, I was in Trinity [College Dublin], studying Modern Languages,' Carol Moffett remembers. 'I took a sabbatical and went home. I went home to be general factotum: floor-sweeper, saleswoman, money-collector. (The last one was quite important. If you don't have much cash flow, you'd better have someone around who's good at getting people to part with their money!) Robert, my brother, inherited my father's flair, so he was the designer. In order to supplement the manufacturing side, I started a retail business selling steel and general engineering supplies.'

Carol Moffett's work in the family firm couldn't have been a greater contrast to Trinity. It couldn't have been harder work. Yet, at the end of the sabbatical, Carol had no desire to continue her studies. What she did have was a growing realisation that, in order to grow the business, the Moffetts needed to find a product that could be made on a production line and sold through a dealer network.

She sees this as a key choice to be made by non-founders who are continuing a family business: do they continue to trade at a small level, providing a living for themselves and a handful of employees, or do they move beyond what the family business has done in the past.

On the face of it, it seems a simple enough choice. Not so, says Carol Moffett. If the second generation decides to expand the business beyond its original shape, they quickly face a wider set of choices:

- They have to decide whether to operate within the home market alone, or export. (Moffett and her brother decided to concentrate on the export market.)
- Carol and Robert hired a young engineering graduate, Jim McAdam, in 1979. He was put in charge of the day-to-day management of the company, leaving Carol free to develop the marketing strategy and Robert to concentrate on design. Carol feels very strongly that while the typical entrepreneur wants to have a finger in every pie, if the business is to grow quickly it is essential to bring in third parties.
- They have to research the market and then produce a product which fits a chosen market niche.

I would add a fourth choice, or issue, here. The next generation has to decide to put at risk what has been achieved up to that point. Any approach that aims to change radically a family business to meet the needs of changing times involves risking a reputation, a market or money that has been built up by the previous generation.

The Moffetts, conscious of all of the risks they faced, took their time about deciding to take any one of them. 'We did our research by slogging around trade shows all over the world,' Carol remembers. 'Gradually, the criteria for a new product came into line. It had to include hydraulics, which was our area of technical competence. It had to be exportable. In 1984, Robert spotted something in the United States (at a trade show) that he thought was a neat idea. A transportable forklift. It was an idea requiring a lot of refinement if it was to suit Irish and European conditions. For example, if you were going to transport your forklift on the rear of a truck, so that [it would be available for use] when you arrived at the place where you were unloading your goods, then the forklift clearly had to be very lightweight. But it also had to be robust enough to carry a two-ton load over a ploughed field.'

The design team quickly produced good working prototypes of what was to become the Moffett Mounty, and launched it on 20 March 1986. On that day, Carol realised they had a winner on their hands because of the tremendous feedback.

In 1986, the family sold fourteen Mountys. In 1987, they sold nineteen machines in the first month. In retrospect, it makes sense for people to buy a forklift they can hang on the rear of the truck that is taking their goods to the delivery sites, but it should not be forgotten that what Moffett's were selling was something that required the customers to change the way they performed a task and did business. Their product did not fit into the existing set-up.

Not only did they change the way in which customers did business at home, Moffetts also tapped into overseas markets that had been unexplored until that point gaining two major customers in the US, namely Home Depot and Lowe's, companies who have big DIY hypermarkets in dozens of states. Their problem was that building products had to be delivered to sites where offloading help was not readily available. A Moffett Mounty, arriving with the truck, changed things. The Moffett Mounty has gone on to become the clear number one in its field worldwide.

'So, from a base in Monaghan most people would have regarded as unfavourable, we created and branded a machine that could sell – and did sell – at premium prices,' Carol comments today. 'The second thing we did wasn't just to refine the original crude idea. We surrounded the product with a package of customer care second to none. We gave such good service that we became locked into the customer – which in turn locked out the competition.'

Service good enough to 'lock out the competition' included built-in training in operation and service for the drivers involved. This proved very important for repeat sales as almost invariably the driver was consulted by management when a decision was being made to add to the fleet. In addition, the first service was free of charge which meant they got the spare-parts business in the future – thus creating another revenue stream.

Looking back, the company believes that branding – establishing the Moffett Mounty as a premium brand in materials handling – was the first key distinguishing point of the vastly expanded business and that exceptional service was the second key point. Tight credit control was the third key point. More than half their production of the new forklift was paid for before it left the factory. (In spite of this tight credit control, they were hit very hard by the Gulf War, when the US market temporarily collapsed, and subsequently had to sell 12.5 per cent of the shares to a venture-capital company; they later repurchased those shares.

Moffett Engineering moved in one generation from a small 'lifestyle' company to a position as Number One in their niche of material handling, worldwide, selling actively in over thirty-five countries. The driving force was Managing Director Carol Moffett who, in the years leading up to the sell-off of Moffett Engineering to PowerScreen in 1998, for a sum believed to have been in the region of £25 million, found herself constantly mentioned in print, with some wonder, as 'the woman running an engineering company exporting worldwide.' Her gender was not something she herself regarded as important.

'There were two occasions when I became aware of it. One of them negative, one positive,' she laughs. 'The negative one is where advisers, whether they're accountants or academics or technical consultants, patronised me. Sorry – tried to patronise me. They didn't succeed, but I sometimes wondered if they take a patronising tone to the whole world, or just to women. It didn't irritate me enough to make me spend time on it, though.

'The other occasion when the fact that I'm a woman in business comes home to me is when I'm overseas on a marketing trip and I get to see the CEO of a big corporation. Occasionally – very occasionally – I have a sneaking impression that one of the reasons I've got in the door to see him (usually it's a him) is that he's intrigued by the notion of a woman from the middle of Ireland flogging forklifts. If being an unexpected female flogger of forklifts helps me flog more forklifts, I don't think I should have a problem with that, do you?'

Carol Moffett and her brother were young, so it is easy to see why they had the vision to broaden a small business into one which would end up making 1,500 machines a year, in two factories – one in Dundalk, the other in Clontibret – and which would have its own selling organisation in the UK and have offices in France, Germany and Spain. In due course, they sold the business, deservedly becoming very wealthy as a result of the sale. Their experience is instructive for other entrepreneurs. If you're going to sell your business, you must build it up as quickly and as profitably as possible, and be confident of your ability to sell it without emotional regrets about possible later generations of the family.

Taking tough decisions in a family business can be greatly helped if the people at the top do not have children. This is not to suggest that families are a bad thing – as a completely involved father of a reasonably large family, I clearly don't think they are. But the phrase 'family business' comes with positive connotations that are not always found in reality, whereas the capacity to take a tiny family operation and turn it into a global empire is easier for someone whose mind is on business rather than on the family.

As was the case with Ray Kroc, who took over McDonald's when it was a one-premises hamburger joint owned by two brothers and built it into a worldwide force. He was not even a member of the McDonald's family and was in his sixties when he identified the potential of the business.

In spite of the fact that, for the larger part of his working life, he had been less than outstanding, Ray Kroc was full of theories, not least of which was that 'the more you sweat, the luckier you get.' This is an instructive idea, but the fact is that some founders are lucky before they work up a great deal of sweat. Timing is one aspect of their luck.

A fast-food outlet with drive-through capacity made sense only at a time in American history when the motor car was becoming the ascendant mode of transport. The development of an overseas McDonald's empire was helped not simply by the onward march of the motor car but also by the speeding up of lifestyles throughout the Western world.

Formal family meals became a casualty of that acceleration, and the yellow McDonald's arches, with their promise of uniformly cooked hamburgers and French fries at cheap prices, quickly delivered, came to symbolise the solution to the problem. The two brothers who had created the family business probably lacked the drive to create the international franchise empire that McDonald's became. While they had high standards, it took someone else to codify those standards into a 'University of Burgerology', where every move, every degree of temperature and every ounce in each serving was part of the unvarying set of procedures which allow McDonald's to provide absolute uniformity of product and service throughout the world.

Kroc was the outsider who took a small family business into the big time. Carol Moffett was the insider who did the same for the business her father started – as was Fred Pressman of Barney's. On this side of the Atlantic, the name Barney's means nothing. In New York, for half a century, the name meant a great deal, particularly to men. The patriarch of this family business, Barney Pressman, started small – at least in terms of premises. He pawned his wife's engagement ring to lease and furnish a small menswear store in Manhattan.

Barney Pressman did not start small in terms of marketing, however. He hired gorgeous models, put them – naked – into wooden barrels emblazoned with his store name and set them to walk Seventh Avenue passing out matchbooks which carried his slogan: 'No Bunk, No Junk, No Imitations'. Barney's specialised in discounted menswear. Pressman shaved anything from 8 per cent to 10 per cent off the recommended retail price – a reduction which at the time meant a great deal to hard-pressed New Yorkers, who needed a good suit in order to look more affluent than they might actually be.

Although the man who wanted to dress better than his budget would allow might go to Barney's, it did not suit the manufacturers of good apparel to have their garments in the window of Barney's carrying a price tag substantially less than the one same garment would bear in Macy's or Lord and Taylor. When Barney began to sell in great volumes, some of those manufacturers found the financial pay-off of retailing through Barney's outweighed the loss of prestige it entailed. Others came under pressure from the more upmarket department stores, which did not want to see the suits they were selling at $40 being discounted to $35 or less in Barney Pressman's tacky store.

Before the war, Barney's did well simply on price. After the war, with men who had seen European tailoring at its best returning to civilian life, Barney's responded by providing tailored suits that were better cut and slightly more fashionable in design than those to be found in the department stores of the day. In the 1950s, Barney's, with the huge lettering of the founder's name over displays of suits, blazers and overcoats, was a household name and a New York institution, situated as it was at Seventh Avenue and Seventeenth Street.

The founder loved the word-of-mouth fame he had achieved, even to the extent of leaping into cabs, demanding to be taken to Barney's and getting right back out of the car if the unfortunate taxi driver asked, 'Where's that?' Pressman believed that a man who was selling more suits than any other single store in the world and employed 150 tailors simply to do the alterations the individual customer might require ought to be known by anybody who claimed to know New York. While Barney was bawling out and abandoning cab drivers who were unwise enough to reveal their ignorance of his emporium, his son, Fred, was toying with the idea of doing law, spending some time in the army and generally giving no indication that he would end up managing Barney's. He was interested in clothes for personal reasons, spending a fortune on the best-crafted menswear available. These clothes never made him look like much, however, partly because he tended to buy suits that were too big for him, and partly because he took no care of them once he had purchased them.

Eventually, the son decided not to go into law but to go into Barney's instead. After he had made this decision, Barney's became an obsession with him, and his preferences and taste in clothing grew into something akin to a personal religion. Take gloves, for example. Fred could dissect a pair of gloves for the best part of an hour, examining the skins and the internal finish. Other staff in

Barney's described his attention to detail and to the finest stitching in invisible parts of a glove as being 'a little psychotic'. Within a few years, he had become an international expert in the structure of a jacket or a pair of trousers and could tell, by pinching a piece of fabric between his fingers, the weight of the cloth to within a fraction of an ounce. That expertise, combined with his almost religious sense of taste and style, inevitably put him on a collision course with what his father had planned when he set up Barney's in the first place.

The older man had wanted to sell in huge quantities at a discount and to sell suits to fat and oddly shaped men and boys who were not being catered for anywhere else. The son not only disliked the odd sizes the store had become known for carrying but was almost personally repelled by the sight of overweight boys being brought in by their mothers for fittings in the store he increasingly wanted to take upmarket. He was just as repelled by his father's loud, brash salesmanship on the floor of the store, and, although he never came into direct conflict with his father about the radical change in style he planned for Barney's, an interesting shot across the parental bows was sent when an ad appeared in the *New York Times* showing a liveried chauffeur opening the door of a Rolls-Royce to allow the car-owner to step out and into Barney's.

Although he was from a strong Jewish tradition, Fred Pressman wanted no part of the discounting culture that had been created by his father out of that tradition. Nor did he want, as customers of his Barney's, the near-social outcasts who had been a mainstay of his father's store: the oddly shaped and the obese. He wanted to sell a better class of merchandise at a higher price to a better class of customer. He began by creating boutiques within the larger store; some of these boutiques expanded until they effectively took over an entire floor.

Fred avoided conflict, particularly of the screaming-match kind his father revelled in, and so, if he thought his father was out to have a fight with him, would physically flee from one area to another in order not to run into him. Contemporaries believed that, although Barney complained about what his son was doing, he never actually stopped any of the significant changes of direction pioneered by Fred but rather went along with them while making – very loud – noises of dissent.

The two men's style with each other was mirrored by their style as bosses. Barney's bark was much worse than his bite; Fred's bite was much worse than his – almost non-existent – bark. One result of this was an almost complete exodus of the lieutenants of the older man after the younger man took over. The older staff, used to hawking their wares in much the same way as Barney did – with a mixture of showbiz, Yiddish and bullying – could adjust neither to the younger man's quieter manner with customers nor to the quite different aesthetics he demanded for the store. Whereas the older salesmen regarded a carpet of torn-off price labels on the shop floor as an indication of how well the store was doing, to Fred Pressman, the same carpet was litter, destroying the pleasing visual impact of the store for the customer.

Fred travelled to Europe as often as he could, to ferret out the best tailors and the most innovative designers. Although Bonwit Teller was the first New York store to carry menswear by Pierre Cardin, Barney's followed swiftly on their heels, offering a much more comprehensive range by the Frenchman. When the Italians eclipsed the French in menswear design, Barney's was one of the first stores to spot what was happening. Indeed, shortly after Giorgio Armani set up in business in 1975, his suits appeared in Barney's: a first in the United States – and a partnership which was to bring huge benefits to both sides.

While Fred Pressman was taking his father's down-market, discount store upmarket and selling goods at astronomical prices, he was maintaining high profits. Each of his buyers quickly learned that the success of the store depended on their negotiating skills, because, although there is a ceiling to what can be charged for any item, if you have pushed the price at which you are buying that item through the floor, you can be sure of high profit margins.

By 1975, Barney's had an annual turnover of $34 million, and a salesman whose commission might be half a dollar for every suit sold could take home $2,500 at the end of a fortnight's work. The company had expanded beyond the dreams of the founder, had attained a cachet the founder's customers would have thought impossible, had attracted a generation of new, young, fashion-conscious, high-spending customers and had generated ever higher levels of profits.

Like Carol Moffett, Fred Pressman had taken his father's business in a direction the parent might not have been able to lead towards himself, but had, in the process, redefined and enlarged the family business's definition of success.

Separated by time and geography and operating in widely different businesses, Moffett and Pressman none-theless demonstrated that the person who originates the business is not necessarily the real founder of that business as a major international entity. They also, in the completely committed, disciplined way they worked, gave the lie to the notion that the heir to the family business is likely to be lazy, self-indulgent and unfocused.

Many heirs to family businesses are lazy, self-indulgent and unfocused. But it sometimes takes more than one generation to reach that point.

4
—

WHEN IT ALL GOES WRONG

The term 'family business' has such a warm, comforting ring to it, conjuring up, as it does, pleasing pictures of mum and dad beavering away, surrounded by their happy, productive offspring, all eyes fixed positively on the future. The reality can be very different. Indeed, murder, mayhem, melodrama and misery, rather than happy collectivism, have characterised several of the most internationally famous family businesses – not to mention some of the smaller ones – in recent years.

The stories of those fatally flawed family businesses are, like the road to hell, paved with good intentions. Take the Koch (pronounced 'coke') family in the United States, where, half a century ago, the patriarch of the family, Fred C., told his young sons that they were to be kind and generous to each other. He warned them that their inheritance of the wealth from his oil business and vast cattle ranches might prove to be a curse. He was so afraid that they would become lazy slobs that he forced them, during their summer holidays from school, to take menial jobs on those ranches.

When his sons were finishing off in university, old Fred must have thought all his tough love had paid off. Indeed, the evidence is that he died happy. At sixty-seven, he was out duck-shooting with a pal when he got off a very good round, turned to his friend to boast about how good a shot he was, and dropped dead.

Act Two of the Koch saga should open with one of the sons taking over as chairman and chief executive of Koch Industries and multiplying the company revenues of $144 million a year a hundredfold. In fact, one of those sons, Charles, did rather better than that. He multiplied the profits a-hundred-and-forty-fold. Working twelve-hour days himself, Charles made it unacceptable not to work on Saturdays. When he proposed to his wife (over the phone), she could hear him flipping the pages of his diary to find a free day for the wedding.

So how did it come about that the people running one of the largest private empires in the United States ended up in the most protracted family dogfight imaginable? The Kochs have been suing each other over sums as small as $700, even though they're worth $2 billion apiece. One of them even subpoenaed his old mother to the witness-stand a few months after she had had a stroke. Four bright, talented men seem to have been turned into inhuman, venomous lifetime litigants by the good fortune of inheriting the family business.

The problem with the Koch family seems to emerge, in part, from the fact that, whereas a workaholic, like Charles Koch, surrounded by other workaholics can be a happy and productive unit, a workaholic with a brother who can't get himself out of bed in the morning tends to be a most unhappy unit. When Charles Koch asked his brother Bill to set up a venture-capital fund for the family, the end result was less than stellar.

Bill Koch defended the fund as having been at least modestly profitable, pointing out that, since his only work experience up to then had been on his father's cattle ranches, expecting outstanding financial performance from him was a bit rich. As the venture-capital saga unfolded, people close to the family began to talk to the media. Since the media could not get family members themselves to talk – the family having strong ideas about privacy – they targeted the next best thing: 'people close to' the family. People close to the Kochs said that Charles had always 'caused problems for Bill'. This had been the judgement of a psychologist who had observed the boys when they were very young, as a result of which Charles had been sent off at the age of eleven to a boarding school, having had the fear of God put into him by his father.

This did not stop Charles from being expelled from boarding school, but it did mean that his father would not take him back into the family but instead sent him, post-expulsion, to live with relatives. This was rather better treatment than another brother, Freddie, had received at the hands of the old man, who had decided when Freddie was a teenager that he was gay, had further decided to break him of his homosexuality by driving him unmercifully during his summer-holiday jobs, had caused him to have a nervous breakdown, had then accused him of stealing money from him and had finally disinherited him.

Bill took a dim view of the fact that another brother, David, got to report, after their father's death, directly to Charles, whereas he, Bill, got to report only to one of the lower orders. Charles took a dim view of the fact that Bill wanted to debate everything for hours instead of asking, when instructed to jump, 'How high?'. David said Bill wanted the fun of negotiation but lacked the business acumen actually to close a deal. Charles said Bill was after his (Charles's) job.

Bill developed a cunning plan. With the support of Freddie and some outside shareholders, he figured he controlled a majority of Koch stock, and called a special board meeting, with the objective of installing new directors, who would influence policy his way and weaken Charles's position. David found out about the plan in time to stymie the move. What followed was twenty solid years of lawsuits, insults and bloody-minded bad behaviour, including the brothers' failure to be civil to each other at their mother's funeral.

It is tempting to take the psychoanalytic route to explain this disaster, which has cost hundreds of millions of dollars, and to suggest that Fred destroyed his children by his own behaviour. Although the patriarch preached mutual regard to his sons, his approach to business veered between secrecy and litigiousness. Secrecy surrounded his friendship and commercial relationship with Stalin. Like Armand Hammer, who also profited out of dealing with Soviet Russia when it was regarded as out of bounds to decent American capitalists, Fred's dealings in Russia were cloaked in mystery but seem to have included helping Stalin to expand his petroleum industry – a financially solid undertaking at a time when, at home, the economy was going through the Depression.

When he came back from Russia, he seems to have spent much of his time in the courts, fighting oil companies, and only occasionally taking time off to do what seems in retrospect to have been a most peculiar version of fathering. Fred pitted one son against another, exiling or humiliating first one and then another, so that every one of his offspring grew up with more understanding of how to be mean-minded and venomous than generous and supportive.

In the advice he gave his children, Fred leaned heavily on Victorian virtues. In the behaviour he provided for them to witness, Fred leaned heavily on values best exemplified by Attila the Hun. It has to be said that in spite of all the litigation and wasted time in the courtroom, Charles has made an incredible success of this business and maybe if his ability had been spotted by his father the family development would have been as spectacular as the business.

If Fred thought his sons would 'Do as I say, not as I do', he seriously miscalculated. 'My father set up the seeds of disaster,' said his son Bill many years after the old man's demise. 'He left the company to all of us, and he wanted us to work together.'

Sounds simple, doesn't it? But in that one sentence can be found the epitaph of so many once-great family businesses. Freda Hayes's father (see Chapter 5) had precisely the same benign wish. In later chapters, I will expand on why this ostensibly simple expectation is the worst possible basis for the continuation of a family business. For now, let's come back to Europe – and a well-dressed murder in Milan.

The hired hit man was very elegantly dressed and did not spoil his image by wearing any kind of mask. Nor did his pistol have a silencer on it. The victim was equally well dressed – as you would expect of one of the Gucci family. Maurizio Gucci, the last family member to sit on the board of Gucci, the internationally famous leatherwear company, was shot at half eight in the morning outside his office in 1995, taking two bullets in the back and one in the head. The assassin calmly got into a car and drove away.

At first, it was suggested that perhaps this was a Mafia execution. Or maybe that Maurizio had been in debt to a loan shark who had ordered that he be 'offed'. But when an arrest was finally made, two years after the crime, the person charged was the victim's estranged wife, Patrizia; the charge was that she had commissioned the murder when in 1994, after twenty-two years of marriage, he had divorced her and taken up with a much younger blonde.

As the months passed before Patrizia came to trial, stories emerged painting her as a woman who might be incarcerated but was nevertheless continuing to wear the furs and jewellery she seemed to see as an aspect of her inner self, and who was reading constantly in prison, insisting that she be supplied only with books that had happy endings. She appeared to have been open and transparent about her plans to give Maurizio an unhappy ending, asking her domestic servants if any of them knew a killer for hire.

When they failed her, she went to a more reliable source of killers: her witch and fortune-teller. The hired killer duly did his job, but in a mad miscalculation, Patrizia Gucci decided to wangle her way out of paying him the full amount she had agreed. The killer began to bad-mouth her to anybody who would listen. His audience included a police informant.

When she was subsequently asked about seeking someone to do away with her late husband, Patrizia pooh-poohed the notion. Well OK, she admitted, she might have articulated a desire to hire a killer, she wasn't daft about Maurizio any more and, hey, you know how it is when you have a bad day? 'Maurizio was my husband. Unfortunately, he was not the man I wanted him to be,' she observed. To the killer, she was not the client he wanted her to be, and his resentment over the money she owed him led to the dawn raid on her home that, two years after the killing, resulted in her ending up in jail. Murder in Milan was a sad and sleazy point for the Gucci empire to have reached.

That empire had started in the mind of a waiter in London. The first Gucci, amassing a nest egg for his future while working as a waiter in London, noticed that the luggage brought to the hotel where he was employed tended to be poorly designed and of even worse craftsmanship. He decided to make high-quality, beautifully constructed luggage – and a decade later began to do so, in his native Italy.

Gucci had spotted a gap in the market, and he began to build a business to fill that gap. In time, he expanded, opening a branch in Rome in the late 1930s and a further branch in New York in 1953. In addition to broadening its geographical base, the company also broadened its product base, its brand appearing on a shoe that was so beautifully designed and made that it is now part of the Museum of Modern Art collection in New York and on a bamboo-handled handbag which became a classic. By the 1960s, the company was also producing silk scarves.

It is difficult to imagine how a company with such a market and such a reputation could be brought to its knees, but it was – and by a problem to which I will have to return again and again in this book. The problem is that of succession and its deadly partner, parental fairness.

Parental fairness was not countenanced at many points in history. Custom and law dictated that everything went, on the father's death, to the eldest son. This system was grossly unfair to the other children – and to the widow – but it had its merits, not least of which was to ensure the continuity of the family business. Where parents try to share and share alike among their children, the results are often catastrophic, most notably in the case of the Irish Famine, where the subdivision of lands into ever-smaller portions over generations contributed to the chaos that followed the potato blight.

Guccio Gucci suffered from a bad sense of parental fairness. He had two sons, and in order to be fair to both of them, he divided his company equally between them: each son received 50 per cent of the shares in the family firm.

Now, that figure has a certain magic to it. Black magic, in my view. The expression 'They divided the business 50–50' has a wonderful, benign ring to it. Unless you're one of those accountants or lawyers who has had to mop up the results of such an even split between family members. If you're one of the mopper-uppers, the very term '50-50' brings on an involuntary flinch.

In Gucci's case, one son, Aldo, like the man in the Bible who takes his talent and parlays it into major financial gain, went to work immediately to build Gucci into an international financial house. Rodolfo, the other brother, frittered away his money and what talent he believed he possessed appearing in second-rate Italian movies. He did not actively get in Aldo's way, however, and so the company grew, and in the process the brand name developed into an asset worth millions.

Then came the handover to the third generation. One of the original 50 per cent shareholdings was divided unevenly among Aldo's children. The other 50 per cent went to the only son of Rodolfo, who was called Maurizio. After this divvy-up, the son of the ne'er-do-well, Rodolfo, had more control over the business than did his three cousins – the offspring of the man who had built it into an international force.

Any kind of business logic would have dictated that the three should get together and come to some sort of agreement. But business logic did not apply. It rarely does in such cases. For instance, one family shareholder involved in a similar situation in a highly successful Irish company announced at a board meeting that he would rather disassemble the business brick by brick in court, even if it cost him everything he had, than come to an agreement with his siblings.

It was much the same with the Guccis. The three sons of Aldo hated each other nearly as much as they hated Maurizio. If 'hate' sounds too strong a word, consider the fact that, at a Gucci board meeting, one director hit another over the head with a tape recorder, using enough force to draw blood. 'Hate' also seems an appropriate word to use to describe the relationship between Paolo and his father, Aldo, which saw Paolo shopping the old man to the Revenue and watching him being led away to prison. Paolo also sued his father, thereby giving him a possibly unique claim to fame as arguably the only man to pay the legal costs of the offspring who was trying to bankrupt him.

Eventually, rather than spend years at board meetings beating each other up with tape recorders, the three decided to flog their half of the business to an American investment house, Investcorp, which had something of a reputation for buying wilting brands and reviving them. The investment house found its usual task was not that easy to accomplish in the case of Gucci, mainly because of difficulty with their partner, Maurizio.

A bad situation was rendered rather more problematic

due to the fact that there had been a few years of promiscuous over-franchising of the famous double-'G' logo. At the beginning of the 1990s, close to 20,000 individual products – ranging from the elegant to the frankly tawdry, from the functional (saddles) to the bar-room accessory (ashtrays) – were licensed to carry this logo. Looking at this mixed bag of tripe, and meeting at every turn with opposition from Maurizio, the investment house decided that the only thing to do was to buy him out completely and install proper financial and administrative control. As a result, Maurizio was the last of the Gucci family to have direct ties to the business.

It was only when those financial controls had been put into place that the Americans realised how bad the situation had become and came to terms with the fact that, in 1993, having gone through the 1980s on the crest of a wave, Gucci was now as near to bankruptcy as made no difference. One of the reasons for this was that Maurizio believed that he and his lifestyle constituted an advertisement for Gucci the company, and so the company had been paying for almost every aspect of that lush lifestyle, one part of which had been the spending of his wife, Patrizia. As the daughter of a cleaning lady, Patrizia had seen it rich and had seen it poor. Unsurprisingly, she found rich the more pleasant of the two – and made no secret of it. 'I'd rather be unhappy in a Rolls-Royce than happy on a bicycle,' she once told an interviewer. Her spending, allied to that of her husband, left a sour taste in the mouths of the new investors.

Once they had full control of the company and some clarity about how and where money was being spent, Investcorp took some obvious steps, like divesting Gucci of a three-masted schooner bought by Maurizio from a Greek multimillionaire and re-hiring key employees who had been fired on a whim by him. Radical action was taken about the over-licensing of the name, and so much discipline was brought to the design, manufacturing, marketing and licensing of the business that, within two years, the value of the corporation had doubled. The firm performed immeasurably better under non-family management than it had when family hands were on the controls. Investcorp subsequently made a handsome profit by selling off Gucci, which is now owned by a series of international investment funds.

James Hanson, a freelance journalist living in Italy who has made a special study of the Gucci near-disaster, maintains that there are many lessons to be drawn from the saga. He says some of these lessons are quite basic: for example, 'If you must divorce, do so as civilly as possible.'

The incivility of Maurizio Gucci's divorce matched much of his previous life. His marriage to Patrizia, who was described by the tabloids as 'a Liz Taylor lookalike', was against the wishes of his father, who characterised her as a gold-digger and tried to involve an archbishop in his efforts to warn Maurizio off marrying her. When that failed, the father told Maurizio he would not permit him to marry until he had passed his university exams – and then hired tutors who were secretly briefed to teach him in such a way that he would fail.

With a father like that, even the most repellent son – and Maurizio seems to have been on a lifelong quest for that title – does not need a wife like Patrizia. But better a high-spending arriviste than an aggrieved ex-wife preparing to do you in. The factor which seems to have tipped Patrizia into her search for the hired gun was her growing conviction that £500,000 a year in alimony was simply not enough to keep her in the style to which she was accustomed. Nor did it help that she figured he planned to disinherit their daughters.

With the last of the Guccis to serve on the board of the family firm dead and buried, and with his wife serving a twenty-year sentence for his murder, the Gucci story suggests that if a dysfunctional PAYE family is bad, a dysfunctional family of heirs to a multinational family business may be a lot worse. Especially if one generation of that family tries to control the next generation via a poorly conceived will.

This has been consciously avoided by my own family, members of which have no problem talking about life after they're gone and a desire to make sure that they don't 'rule from the grave'. The people who are alive and running the business have to be able to make decisions that are right for the business on that particular day. And that could include selling it.

Many older generations within family businesses have very definite ideas on how the business should be run – and these may extend to how it should be run when they're gone. This benign intention can manifest itself in one of two damaging ways. The first, typically, is where a founder ostensibly hands control to the younger generation but cannot in fact let go of it. As soon as a crisis or an emergency erupts, the founder, driven by the conviction that they know best, gets back into hands-on management.

When you hand over a business, you should – assuming you have someone in the next generation who can handle it – hand over all of the shareholding and the legal control of the firm to that person. Just as importantly, you should hand over the actual control of the business as well, rather than hanging around the office interfering. Your relationship with your offspring should be good enough to ensure that your input and influence is still there but can be turned on and off by the next generation like a tap. If there is a problem, the new MD should not immediately think, 'Well, the last thing I'm going to do is go to the old man on this.' On the contrary, they should think, 'On my way home, I'll drop in on the old man and see what he thinks.' If the old man can develop that kind of relationship, he – and his successors – will have the best of both worlds. The second way that older generations can set out, with the best of intentions, to 'guide' their successors – but in the process can end up crippling them and their business – is through a controlling will.

Many wills rule from beyond the grave. For instance, some wills insist that inheritors may sell their shareholding only to other family members or must share the proceeds of any sale among all siblings. Leaving shareholdings with all sorts of provisos may be very admirable and may suit the day when the will is being written but, five, ten or fifteen years down the road, may act as a straitjacket when the heir is trying to run the business.

'Think carefully,' commentator James Hanson tells the owners of family businesses, 'about the damage you may do to your heirs and to your company by leaving a bad will. The weakness of family ownership becomes manifest in the third generation.'

All this advice could usefully have been taken on board by the successful second generation at Barney's in New York. As we have seen, Fred Pressman had succeeded his father, the original 'Barney', and had successfully steered the organisation in a different direction, relying on quality imported menswear from Europe's leading tailors rather than the more simple 'unique selling proposition' – of selling heavily discounted branded suits – that his father had relied on.

Then along came Fred's two sons, the more creative of them, Gene, making his mark on the store from the mid-1970s. Barneys had started in the 1920s; what had taken half a century to build into a massive, solidly established success story took roughly a decade to plunge into penury, once the third generation had got their hands on it.

Just as Fred had been somewhat ashamed of his father's manner of trading, so Gene, in particular, was somewhat ashamed of his father's limited vision. Gene decided that Barney's should sell women's fashions. But not just any women's fashions. It should sell the most expensive, the most luxurious, the most de luxe women's fashions, from the best designers in the world. Fred, who permitted the expansion into womenswear, is believed to have felt that if a certain initial exclusivity were attached to the women's clothes sold by Barney's, that exclusivity would later somehow flow on to somewhat less expensive ranges.

It worked the other way. As time went on, Gene and his brother Robert became increasingly concerned that their upmarket ranges of designer clothes would be tainted by association with the old Barney's, and so their hearts became set on opening a completely new store in central Manhattan which would, from the front door to the topmost ceiling, be an object lesson in elegance.

Instead, the new store, at 660 Madison Avenue, was a case study in drunken-sailor spending. On the night in

1993 when it opened, VIPs wandered throughout a store which had cost $267 million to fit out. As silver leaf tarnishes, what looked like silver leaf on the walls was in reality platinum. There was platinum and real goatskin on the walls, mother-of-pearl shelves and silk curtains, exotic woods like bleached bubinga and a Carrera marble mosaic in the centre of the main floor. If there was an off-key note in the celebration, it was provided by the escalators, which worked but emitted a mad, keening wail, as if predicting a dire future for the place.

Fred Pressman and the escalators seemed to be in agreement. 'In five generations, I don't know if we'll be able to pay for this,' he told a magazine shortly after the opening. Three years later, he died, at the age of seventy-three, having lived to see the company his father had founded seek Chapter 11 status: protection from creditors under the bankruptcy code.

Fred had pushed aside his own father and rebuilt the company around his own ideas, and his father had made noises of dissent but had not presented implacable opposition to what Fred had wanted to do. So, when Gene came along with his even grander ideas – each of them a quantum leap from what Fred had set out to achieve in his day – and when those ideas were supported by Bob, the finance man, Fred seems to have shrugged and lived in hope.

He shouldn't have. Nor should he have believed that Gene had the flair, discipline and focus on profit he himself possessed. Gene's grasp of the realities of the clothing business eroded, rather than developed, as he gained power, so that towards the end, he was more absorbed by the desire to teach lessons to the Japanese investors on whom the Pressman brothers depended for their futures than by the desire to rescue the family business and set it on a rational footing.

This is a possibility that parents, whether of the first or second generation, do not seem to be good at accommodating: that one or more of their children may be spoilt, either by having a fundamentally rotten nature – as some of his contemporaries believed Maurizio Gucci had – or by a childhood where one or both parents are absent at work most of the time, where one or both parents are preoccupied, if not obsessed, by work all of the time and where one or both parents imagine that they can send their children to the best schools and indulge them with the best playthings instead of being present and involved in their upbringing.

The Pressman brothers of the third generation were a lethal combination. Gene had flair and the arrogance that goes with it. Robert seems to have perceived himself to be in a bizarre game of 'chicken'. He appears to have seen it as his job to get the money to enable Gene's big ideas to be brought to fruition, lest it in some way be seen as Bob's fault that this third-generation Barney's genius was hampered, inhibited or thwarted in the expression of his brilliance by his more workaday brother. Whatever financial rectitude Robert had in the beginning – and it would appear that he had quite a lot– by the end he was on a robbing-Peter-to-pay-Paul merry-go-round devoted mainly to salvaging family members' personal property from the maelstrom into which the entire business was descending.

Maurizio Gucci did not need a brother in order to prove fatal for the family business. He had an infinite capacity to snatch defeat from the jaws of victory. Starting out with invaluable advantages, including looks, charm, wealth and family reputation, he managed to bring the family business very close to destruction while at the same time making himself so obnoxious that his first wife arranged to have him killed and the partner with whom he was living at the time of his murder in Milan stayed away from his funeral. Indeed, so many of his former friends and relatives decided not to attend the funeral that one observer commented there were more TV cameras than people in the church.

It has often been said, ironically, that if you want to live a long time, the essential step to take is to choose your parents. Looking at the fate of Barney's and Gucci, it seems inescapable that any family firm with a concern for its longevity should look, not to the parents, but to their offspring, and should make sure that the second or third generation do not have a barely concealed yearning to relocate to Skid Row. While family businesses nearer to home have not yet had murders or litigation running into billions, several have gone through fairly public tribulations that they would undoubtedly have wished to avoid.

The key lesson any family business can learn from the crashes of such high-flyers is that, if the people currently running the business do not wish to sell it, they should at least ensure that, when it is time to relinquish control, that control is handed over carefully and to the right person. The worst option – which is, unfortunately, the option most frequently exercised – is to divide the future control of the family business evenly among the next generation.

5

UNCLE BEN AND THE WOOLLEN MILLS

For years, Dunnes Stores' slogan and logo were familiar to Irish consumers: the 'Better value beats them all' slogan; the St Bernard logo, which some said was modelled on Marks & Spencer's St Michael brand.

You could interpret both the slogan and the logo whichever way you wanted, because the Dunnes family did little in the way of PR. They saw off several other grocery chains while always maintaining their business's textile arm, which supplied generations of Irish families with cheap imported anoraks and runners. There was a harsh, mass-produced air to the operation, but, that said, Dunnes Stores was a national success story.

The company had been started by Ben Dunne, Senior. His son, Ben Dunne, Junior, was a significant figure in the business during the 1970s, but, outside of those who dealt with him directly or played golf with him, was not publicly known in the way that, for example, fellow supermarket tycoon Feargal Quinn of Superquinn was known around the same time. Even Maurice Pratt, the marketing man who fronted for the now-sold Quinnsworth chain in TV ads, was better known than the multimillionaire whose name had been co-opted for the central brand offered by Dunnes Stores.

The first time Dunne Junior sprang to national prominence was when he fell foul of the law on a trip to Florida in February 1992. Dunne, having sniffed cocaine, seems to have threatened to jump from a high balcony near the hotel room he was sharing with a woman from an escort agency. Returning home, he performed a tour de force of openness, meeting journalists and taking the blame for everything that had happened without equivocation. Having always, as a clan, avoided personal media exposure, the Dunnes had the odd experience of seeing Ben, badly caught out, emerging as something of a hero within the media for the completely upfront nature of his confession.

Dunne's new-found fame was to continue throughout the 1990s, as it emerged that some of his financial dealings were interesting rather than orthodox. The times were against him, the nineties becoming the decade of the tribunals, as one investigation after another was set up to investigate possible malfeasance by politicians during the previous twenty years. One of those bodies, the McCracken Tribunal, found that Dunne had made payments to a former Fine Gael minister, Michael Lowry, who was then a supplier of refrigeration equipment to Dunnes Stores, in ways designed to help Lowry evade tax. Sometimes the payments took the form of offshore deposits. On one occasion, Dunnes Stores picked up the bill, amounting to almost £400,000, for an extension to Mr Lowry's home. This was creatively allocated, in Dunnes Stores' books, to work on the Ilac Centre in Dublin.

If unusual payments to Michael Lowry kept Ben Dunne in the spotlight, unusual donations to Charles Haughey brought him centre stage in another tribunal – the Moriarty Tribunal, set up in September 1997, following the report of the McCracken Tribunal. Justice Moriarty set out to investigate payments to former Taoiseach Charles J. Haughey and Michael Lowry and to track any connection between those payments and any political decision made or influenced by either man which might have benefited a person or company making such a payment.

The stories about the payments to the former Taoiseach were invariably accompanied by pictures of the supermarket scion bending over to shake the hand of the much shorter and lighter politician at some function. They seemed to underscore the strangeness of the relationship behind the gifts which, according to Ben Dunne's account, had been handed over on impulse, when, visiting him after a golf game, he had thought Charlie Haughey was a bit depressed and, by way of alleviating that depression, pressed a couple of cheques extracted from the back pocket of his golf trousers on the leader of the Fianna Fáil party. On receiving the cheques, the latter, according to Dunne's account, said 'Thanks, Big Fella'. It was a one-liner with legs, and it ran and ran.

One of the people infuriated from the beginning by the possibility that C. J. Haughey might have been the beneficiary of Dunnes Stores' money was Ben's older sister, Margaret Heffernan. Heffernan, a vividly dressed, dark-haired woman married to a surgeon, has a passion for her family equalled only by her passion for her family business. Although not all of her children have gone into that business, they each spent time at the coalface during their summer holidays from school, when their mother insisted they must experience, for several weeks each year, the toughest low-level jobs the stores had to offer. Margaret Heffernan's own organisational and motivational skills are not in doubt. She has been a key figure in many massive charitable campaigns, serving not as one of the 'ladies who lunch' but as one of the ladies who kick ass and get results. She also bridles at any suggestion that Dunnes Stores is a less rewarding employer than any of its competitors and she has been instrumental in recent years in the chain's move upmarket.

When Heffernan heard that her brother might have given Haughey a cheque or two, she took herself speedily out to the former Taoiseach's home in Kinsealy on the north side of Dublin to get the facts. She failed. Even this remarkably direct woman's questioning failed to elicit the details which were later to emerge about her brother's generosity to a man who had, it is believed, earned her loathing many years previously, when he had, with manifest contempt, ordered that a display of cheap Dunnes Stores shirts be removed from an exhibition in which he was involved. (When it was revealed, in 1999, that considerable sums donated by men such as Ben Dunne had been paid by Mr Haughey to the Parisian shirt-makers Charvet, there was much sardonic comment to the effect that, if Ben Dunne was keeping him solvent, the least Charlie could have done was to wear Dunnes Stores shirts.)

The tensions of the early nineties eventually resulted in the effective expulsion of Ben Dunne from the business set up by his father. On the face of it, the story seems like a tale of 'Tough Elder Sister Sees Off Spoilt Brat Younger Brother'.

There is much more to the Dunnes Stores saga than generational misunderstanding – although there is an age gap between Ben Dunne and Margaret Heffernan, the most visible siblings of a much larger brood. More significantly, those two are the surviving siblings of a brood some members of whom have died at a much younger age than might have been expected, having had long, losing battles with alcohol before they died. Nor is it valid to assume that Dunne should never have gone into the business or been allowed to become so powerful.

The fact is that Ben Dunne, in common with some of his generation who are now dead, had a huge amount of ability. A comment that a period in jail would have done him good has been attributed to Margaret Heffernan. Those close to her point out that she very likely meant the comment literally: that a period in jail would have separated him from the pattern of high living which she would regard as having clouded his judgment and having led him into situations which did neither his reputation nor the reputation of the chain any good. Although she has never talked publicly about her brother, it is known that she has never dismissed the business competence of 'Bernard', as she always calls him. (Similarly, Ben, in the middle of the controversy, announced publicly that he liked his sister.) Just as some of their siblings were brilliant buyers – except when alcohol came into play – so Bernard was a highly effective manager of the business – except when drugs or the desire to be well-got with what were regarded as the VIPs of the time came into play.

From the outside, it is possible to suggest that Ben Dunne suited the shape Dunnes Stores was in during the seventies and early eighties. The times that were in it condoned, or gave the appearance of condoning, creativity in tax avoidance and tax evasion. Dunnes Stores had a long reputation, which predated young Ben's arrival on the scene, of driving such a hard bargain with major suppliers as to make those suppliers virtually – and subserviently – dependent on the Dunnes for survival.

As some of the second generation failed, Margaret Heffernan seems to have moved into a closer and more powerful position within the family hierarchy. If she failed to get the full truth out of Charlie Haughey, she nonetheless made it clear, in her evidence to the subsequent tribunal, that Dunnes Stores would never have given such moneys if she had had anything to do with it and that, now that the reins were more firmly in her hands, there would be no further payments along those lines. If Ben had been in tune with the moral melodies of the seventies and early eighties, Margaret was strong on the harmony line at the end of the nineties.

None of which answered the two questions which inevitably arise in relation to this state of affairs. First, were the problems of the second generation of Dunnes Stores the result of involvement in the family business? Second, would the business survive in family ownership into the third generation?

Because of the relative secrecy of the Dunne family, in spite of their recent media exposure, it will never be easy to answer the first question. Alcoholism tends to run in families – although whether genetics or some other factor is the cause has yet to be proved. To be brought up by a tough, demanding father with his eye permanently on the bottom line and his focus permanently on profit may not be easy. Nonetheless, it would be difficult to argue that the early death of some of the second generation of that family should be attributed to upbringing when it is perfectly clear that other members of the same generation have been remarkably successful both in business and family terms.

Even Ben Dunne represents something of a case study in something that is arguably more difficult than grace under pressure: public rehabilitation under pressure.

On the other hand, just as the old joke has someone in the audience of a high-flown speech mutter that, while they're still confused about the subject, they're now confused at a higher level, it could be argued that, for some of the second generation in a family business like Dunnes Stores, the pressure and competitiveness inherent in involvement from an early age ensures that any failure will be fairly intense and potentially dramatic. But would those wounded in the fray have preferred to be born into a family where both parents are PAYE earners? And would it have made much difference to their eventual fate?

It can also be argued that the pressures on the second generation of developing a business beyond the point to which the first generation has brought it can bring out the worst in the younger brigade. For those who came into the Blarney Woollen Mills business, this does seem to have applied.

Blarney Woollen Mills had an annual turnover of £50 million in 1998. It also had major retail outlets in Dublin, Blarney, Killarney and Kilkenny. In addition, it owned two hotels, a mail-order business, a knitwear factory and some investment properties. We know this because the information came out in court, when a member of the board of the company, Michael O'Gorman, went to the High Court to stop members of the Kelleher family from removing him (their brother-in-law) from the board of directors. In court, a picture was painted of a family that was so badly split down the middle that the chief executive believed the only way to get her ideas past the board was to get someone else to propose them.

It was a situation that would have made the founder of the company turn in his grave. Christy Kelleher had been a devout believer in family businesses, quoting as role models the empires built by families like Levi Strauss. During the year when he was praising Levi Strauss (which has subsequently experienced its own setbacks), Christy Kelleher was presiding over a business that involved three of his four sons, each of his three daughters and a few of his in-laws. This business had grown from tiny beginnings, as a knitwear and souvenir shop in a thatched cottage on wheels outside Blarney Castle, and was still expanding. Sibling rivalry caused the splitting up of what had been a glowing family business.

It was a sad souring of Christy Kelleher's dream. The founder of the family business had gone to work in Mahony's Woollen Mills in Blarney when he was thirteen. He had risen to supervisor level by the time he left, more than twenty years later, to become an insurance salesman – and a lot more besides. Kelleher was a workaholic who sold apples in the autumn, charged for taking sporting teams to the venues for their matches, ran movies in the cinema he purchased and turned it into a ballroom at weekends. When he had nothing better to do, he sold vegetables.

But he was also observant. He observed the constant and growing flow of tourists arriving at Blarney Castle, decided to get a piece of that action, hired local knitters to make up jumpers, built his mobile thatched cottage and had a turnover of £14 on his first day of trading. That same year, his daughter Freda turned sixteen, left school and went into the business. The cinema was transformed into a knitwear factory, and in 1974 Christy bought the mill that had employed him for twenty-two years.

As she had started in the company at such a young age, Freda seemed the obvious choice as managing director, and in due course she took on that role, her father encouraging other members of the family to move from the jobs they had at the time and join the family firm. Christy seems to have been able to control the inevitable sibling rivalries during his lifetime. It was only at the beginning of the nineties, after his death, that these rivalries became ungovernable.

Although Freda Hayes had much experience running the company, there was much dissent at some of her decisions, not least of which was to bring in outside expertise to help take the family business into the new century. There was much manoeuvring at board level, and Freda lost out. In 1992 she resigned, taking with her some £1.5 million – her share of the empire her father had hoped would long outlast him. She used this money to set up her own company, which now owns a major hotel, as well as stores in Dublin, Cork, Galway and Bunratty, and does business worth in the region of £10 million a year.

After Freda Hayes left, her sister Marian O'Gorman took over as chief executive, but the disagreements between family members continued long after her departure, with factions developing among the remaining siblings. The final break-up of the company had, in one sense, been flagged by Freda Hayes's departure. It was yet another case study of hope triumphing over reason and of a man projecting his own single-mindedness about his family business on to members of the clan, who never approached that standard.

Today, looking back at her father's hopes and dreams,

Freda Hayes maintains that the link between her father buying the mill in 1975 and bringing in family members over the next three years may have been very unfair on many of those family members.

The tendency to bring family members in at the top rather than at the bottom is a recurring problem in family businesses. For those who are brought in, this can cause a problem throughout their lives. Because they arrive at a time when the business is well established and successful, they never remember the poor days. Indeed, quite frequently, founders themselves develop merciful amnesia about those difficult days.

Perhaps because she joined the firm not long after its foundation, Freda Hayes remembers the tough early days very vividly. 'There would be weeks when we didn't have the money to buy yarn to keep the factory going for next Friday,' she recalls. 'I had to drive up to Tullamore Yarns with money to fill up the boot of my car with yarn to keep the machines going the following day. I learnt a lot about survival in the first five or six years. Even the banks – our own AIB – told us, "Forget it. Throw in the towel."'

Her father, whom she describes as 'a visionary', left his paid job in New Ireland Assurance in 1976 and took early retirement. 'I was running the company anyway, which suited him,' she recalls. 'He never had an office, never had an executive role within the company. He left me to run the company. He wouldn't even chair the meetings; I chaired the meetings.

'He believed in consensus, which I didn't always agree with. If we couldn't agree on something, he'd keep hammering away until we agreed, even if it wasn't on the thing we originally started with, and basically, if there was a serious problem within the family (and there were, even when he was alive), he was the paternal figure.'

Freda Hayes believes this benign paternal insistence on consensus – and quite often consensus around a decision Freda had made – may have initiated a bad pattern. More naked disagreement at the time might have forced the other members of the family to do something about it, might even have forced them to reach – much earlier and at a less damaging time – the impasse reached later.

'I run my own business now, and I say to my son that I intend to sell it in due course. That if he decides tomorrow morning to go to train in Dunnes Stores or somewhere and learn to be a retail manager and in ten years' time is absolutely brilliant, I might change my mind. But he's not interested in the retail business and I certainly wouldn't encourage him, because I do think that if you're coming into a business that's already established by your parent, you do find it very hard to build your own confidence. You need to make loads of mistakes to gain confidence. But it's not a good place to be making mistakes in a family business, where someone's going to say, "Oh well, he's the boss's son."'

The lesson is clear. It is that, in business terms, Yeats's line asking that the beloved 'Tread softly, for you tread on my dreams' should never be used by the founders of businesses. They have no right to wish their dreams onto their successors, nor to demand that their successors subordinate their own dreams to the family business. So, if you're the founder of a business – or even, with your spouse, a joint founder – think long and hard before you make the assumption that what you have created is a family business. It's your business, your dream and your asset. The best option for the long-term happiness of family members and employees alike may be for you to sell the business and stake your kids to start up their own enterprises.

Some businesses become family businesses because the founders can't face the empty nest. They love the idea that their children will in due course take over from them. They apply benign pressure and, if you point this out, they deny it. Not at all, they say. Of course they'd be happy if Son Number 1 became a graphic artist rather than general manager of the family business. It wouldn't cost them a thought if Daughter Number 1 opted never to set foot in it. No hassle if the rest of the kids all went and did something quite different. They wouldn't dream of influencing them in any way.

They believe what they're saying, but they don't always examine the evidence that contradicts their claims. 'My parents delude themselves that they never influenced my choice of career,' one second-generation executive in a family business told me. 'They don't realise that, especially when you're an only child, if both your parents are involved in the family business, whether it's a local pub or a convenience store, you're steeped in the folklore of the business and it has a subliminal pull on you.'

There are too many more alternatives which are healthier. For the family and for the business.

6
—

Assumptions from Birth

When you're part of a family which has owned a successful business for several generations, you grow up surrounded by assumptions. People make those assumptions about you long before you're old enough to know about it. I'm told that, as soon as my mother left hospital after giving birth to me, I had to be brought into the newspaper offices in Academy Street and shown off to the staff. As soon as I was old enough to do a summer job, it was assumed that this summer job would happen in the newspaper, and someone on the staff would always remark, only half-joking, 'You'll be the boss some day. I hope you'll look after me. I'd better stay in with you.' You quickly get to the stage where that kind of comment becomes one of your own assumptions. You start to believe it. You say to yourself, 'Yeah, that's right – I'll do that when I become the boss.'

Another assumption that surrounded the children in our house when we were growing up was that we were millionaires. Other kids would call after us in sing-song voices, 'The Crosbies are million-aires.'

It never made sense, that catch-cry, to any of us, with our mother saying, 'Go easy on the marmalade. Do you realise this week's groceries cost me twenty-three pounds?' We never had fancy cars. We did have a big house, but then, we had a big family. It was very much a family house:

it was not full of antiques. We also had a boat. My father, George Crosbie, had bought it second-hand, when it was already twenty years old. In common with most of our neighbours at the time, we didn't take foreign holidays; instead, we rented a house in Myrtleville near Crosshaven for a month in the summer.

Just as some kids know that their family members tend to work on the buses or in the brewery, the Crosbie kids knew that their father, uncles and grandfather worked in 'the paper'. And I, as the eldest son, knew from my earliest days that I would also work in the paper, and probably end up as CEO, if not chairman, of the company. This was an inevitability rather than a blessing or an imposition.

When we went into the offices to see my father, the printers would make up a metal slug with my name on it. But that was about the extent of the 'romantic attachment' between any of my generation and the business until we actually became involved in it. To this day, I am struck, when I take visitors around the print room and the other areas through which the paper moves before it hits the streets, by the impact the machinery, the noise and the smells have on them. It seems to catch the imagination of outsiders much more than it ever caught the imagination of us, the insiders – in the early days, at least. The truth of the matter is that I never really developed a love for newspapers until I went to work in newspapers as an adult.

In the interim, the family business did not impinge that much on any of us. My father did not bring home his work, nor was it discussed much at home. His side of the business was the commercial side: advertising and marketing. From my own point of view, as a child, this aspect of the business was the least interesting.

There were lines of demarcation even at director level. Production was the responsibility of my father's cousin Ted, who was an engineer. Editorial matters were looked after by my uncle Donal, who had trained as a barrister. Family members did not tend to cross these clearly established lines; with hindsight, this may have been a mistake. When I joined Examiner Publications, it was a given that I would work on the advertising side, because that was where my father worked. No particular thought was given to my aptitude. I would probably have been more suited to the editorial side, whereas one of my cousins – who is not in the business any more but who went into the editorial side because that was where his father worked – would, in my opinion, have been even better in advertising and PR.

In my teens, the prospect of going into the paper was not much of an issue for me. I was much more interested in playing rugby and chasing girls. (This was after a brief period when I had a miniature altar in my room and convinced everybody, including myself, that I would end up as a priest.) If asked what I was going to be, I said was going to work in the *Examiner*. Interestingly, if one of my five kids is asked the same question, only one, at the time of writing, says he is going to work in the paper. The one great thing about the newspaper business as opposed to many other businesses is that there are very few types of character for whom there is not a suitable space.

There was always going to be space – and space at the top – for me in Examiner Publications. Unfair with regard to my sisters, two of whom are older than me? Absolutely. But then, our family business has survived to this point through a combination of luck, convenient death and male chauvinism. Since Thomas, the first Crosbie in the *Examiner* story, died, the paper has come through famine, civil war, two world wars, petrol shortages and five generations of Crosbies without ever missing an edition. Significantly, too, after those five generations, the paper has only three shareholders. The first son in each generation always got the shares – and was going to get the shares even if he was manifestly unsuited to owning a piggy bank filled with pennies. The eldest might be female — and was, in my family's case. It was pure luck that, in each generation, there was somebody among those first sons who was tolerably able to run the organisation.

People who don't come from family businesses find this outrageous and tell me that I was unjustly privileged (correct) and born with a silver spoon in my mouth. I always say, 'What did you expect me to do, spit it out?' What matters is not what you inherit but what you do with it.

I left school at seventeen, took two weeks' holidays and then went into the family business. A programme was made out for me. I would spend three years working in various companies – at the *Examiner's* expense – where I would learn about business. It was, in a way, a practical, experiential alternative to spending the same period of time in a university.

I started off with a five-month stint in Guinness's, at James's Gate, working in the management-services department. I then went, on Guinness's suggestion, to Park Royal in London, where I worked as an under-brewer. This was in effect a cadet position. Head brewers were – and are – gods in that business. Although the brewing industry may not seem to relate to newspapers, the objective was for me to learn how any business operates.

In 1973, I went to Irish Marketing Surveys, which was run by John Meagher and Robin Addis. I worked there for a summer, doing field research and collating. I also worked in the department that designs the questionnaires, which was very helpful later, when I was assessing the joint National Media Research, to which the *Irish Examiner* and all the other newspapers contribute and from which they draw market information.

Then I went to Arks Advertising for a year and a half, working in various departments. Many of the people who were with me there at the time moved on to set up their own media companies or to run industrial firms. It is part of the nature of advertising agencies that there tends to be a high upward and outward mobility of creative and other staff. After that, it was overseas, with a stint at the *Sacramento Bee* – a wonderful newspaper run by a famous family named the McClachies. The older proprietor character in the television series *Lou Grant* was based on old Mrs McClachie. In the series, she came across as a wonderful woman, and she was a wonderful woman in real life too. The paper's logo was a bee, originally drawn by Walt Disney. It was and is a great newspaper.

I worked at the *Sacramento Bee* for the best part of a year, as a trainee in the area of advertising and telesales. It was a very lonely year for a twenty-one-year-old who knew nobody. All I had was a job. But I was already noting where things were done well, and one of the things done very well at the Sacramento operation was sales training. I sub-sequently brought their sales trainer over to Ireland to train tele-ad people at the *Examiner*.

I came back to Ireland in 1976, staying for four years. Then, in 1980, I went to Australia. I worked with the

Courier Mail in Brisbane. Homesickness was less a problem this time, partly because I went out there with my Australian girlfriend of the time. I was being paid by the *Examiner* but worked at one of the radio stations owned by the *Courier Mail* in Brisbane.

While I was doing this 'degree course', I had doubts about my own future. I found I didn't want to take on the CEO's job, when it came up, unless I had first proven to my own satisfaction that I could do it: that I could demonstrate to other potential employers that I was worth employing. When I was in Australia, I was offered a good enough job to justify abandoning my place in the family business if I wanted to, and in a sense, that job offer allowed me to come home with a greater sense of equanimity. The offer showed me I could have been a contender somewhere other than the *Examiner;* it told me I could have been CEO at the *Examiner* even if my name wasn't Crosbie.

Then I came back to the paper and started to work my way up. Looking back over the thirteen years I spent in different areas of the business before taking over, I remember that, in every one of the businesses in which I worked, issues surfaced that were to surface later at the *Examiner*. It is quite difficult to disentangle the issues that are intrinsically 'family' from the issues that occur in any business. For example, you get personality conflicts in any business. You get bullies and cowards in any business. You get time-servers and peacekeepers and iconoclasts in any business. The issues and the characteristics are common to all industries, and the methods of coping with them are not that different in a family business. The bully has to be faced down; the peacekeepers and time-servers have to be positioned in areas that do not require innovation or courage.

There is an extra perceived difficulty in family businesses, where obnoxious character traits may be allowed to manifest themselves longer than might happen in a public company, because the person being obnoxious is the head of the family or is clearly placed close to the top in terms of succession. I talk of this as a perceived, rather than a real, difficulty because, in listening to management consultants who conduct communications audits across the full span of company types, it is clear that the same behaviours surface in all kinds of companies. There are pecking orders and cliques everywhere: that's the nature of things. In family firms, however, there is a neat dynastic – even genetic – explanation for them. In such firms there is also a matching excuse for not doing anything about these problems, as exemplified by the attitude that, 'Oh, I knew his grandfather, and he was exactly the same – no talking to him.'

In my first year back in Cork, I worked as an advertising sales rep, selling advertorial features. I have been up the sides of mountains, selling one-inch single-column ads to fellows sitting on tractors. I remember slogging around selling forty one-inch ads for a local festival.

'I'm Alan Crosbie from the *Cork Examiner,* which I'm sure you're familiar with,' I would say. 'We've been supplied with a list by the organisers of *Féile na Máille* of people they feel would be interested in supporting a feature we're doing. It'll comprise pictures, editorial and advertising. What would you like to say in your ad?'

I learnt early that if you say, 'Would you like an ad?' they say no, whereas if you ask them what they want in it, they agree. But I also learnt the key thing about newspapers: they are in the business of making connections. They are supposed to make connections for people – and not just through editorial. Advertising serves that connection function, too, as does every human contact – every interface – between the staff of the newspaper and its public.

In the eighties, the *Examiner*, in common with many other newspapers, walked into a wall. All the numbers – readership, turnover, profit – began gradually to sink. During the ten years that followed, the paper made losses. If we had been a publicly quoted company, a massive public purge would undoubtedly have taken place. But one of the great advantages of family businesses is that they tend to take the long view.

Not long ago, I was listening to a group of people in their thirties who had, the previous year, sold a large chunk of equity in their company to a venture-capital house. The conflict between the original shareholders and the new shareholders was coming into sharp relief at the time I was listening to the original founders. Basically, the original shareholders wanted to build up something, create a long run of excellent products and pull together a long-term team, while the new shareholders wanted profits and profit growth from quarter to quarter. The two groups' central objective was, in theory, more or less the same, but their time-lines were so different as to render the ostensibly common interest between the two sides meaningless.

One of the great strengths of family firms is that, in bad times, they tend to gird their loins and dig in for the long haul. They have been around for a long time, surviving recessions, so they figure they can take a few years of pain until the good times start to roll again.

In some cases, family firms also have a profound, ingrained sense of connectedness to their staff and customers. The most notable example of connectedness to customers happened during the Depression in the United States, when farmers went bankrupt in their thousands. Other farm-equipment corporations, acting logically, foreclosed when payments stopped being made by the farming community. The exception was the John Deere company, which made the decision that it had to share the pain its customers were going through – and renegotiated its hire-purchase agreements so that cash-strapped farmers were able to hold on to their machines even though they could not, at that time, afford to pay for them. It was a move which stood to John Deere for generations thereafter, but it was classic family-firm thinking, rather than a decision motivated by the desire to maintain a good public image.

Family businesses in general tend to be less profitable than other kinds of business. Family firms take a long time to build, but building them, rather than satisfying the short-term dividend needs of a group of shareholders, is usually the key objective. In operating to these different objectives, family firms are greatly helped by the fact that they do not have a public AGM at which they have to show shareholders what they have achieved. A public company has to prove, every single year, that it is profitable; a family firm does not.

So even though the *Examiner* was losing money, my predecessor (rightly) invested heavily in technology, partly because he was an engineer and the production side of the business was Ted Crosbie's first love. But it was also a demonstration of his faith in the long-term future of the business. This faith tends to characterise family businesses that survive past the third generation. Although very few do survive past that generation, the minority who make it to the fourth – or in our case, the fifth – generation tend to see themselves as having responsibilities to more than the bottom line.

This is both a positive and a negative cast of mind. When top management gets the idea that quality of product, or continuation of family tradition, or good corporate citizenship, rather than profit, is the chief issue, the company is beginning to go down the tubes, because it has forgotten the central commercial truth that the business of business is business.

We have already seen examples of companies which have lost sight of this obvious point: Barney's, where personal vanity, which manifested itself in the form of gross overspending on peripherals, became the central issue, and Blarney Woollen Mills, where family squabbles distracted attention from the business itself. But this failing is not confined to family businesses. On the contrary. Read any of the books by the business gurus of the 1970s or 1980s, and you will often find some of the business heroes of the day describing in their own words the seeds of their companies' failure. At the time those words were written, the companies were hugely successful, but they have since disappeared because they concentrated on some pet aspect of their industry and left the wider business to fend for itself.

The airlines provide copious examples of this phenomenon. The pioneers of cheap flights have too often operated as if the David-and-Goliath position they had at the start of their operations would continue – and have found that belief to be sadly unrealistic. But then, overly rigid thinking into the future based on the present is a human failing which crops up again and again in history, most frequently in that most family of businesses, royalty.

Much the same rational but flawed thinking appeared in the area of planning in Dublin at the end of the last century. A major study into public and private transport correctly predicted that, in the twentieth century, the capital would have problems coping with the fallout from transporting its population from home to work and shops, and back again. The only thing the survey got wrong was what it saw as the central consequence of this trend: horse shit. Given that the horse was the major means of propulsion and that Dublin's population was increasing, if you multiplied the predictable growth in horse numbers by the predictable output, the study concluded that Dubliners, by mid-century, were going to be up to their knees in the stuff.

What the planners did not reckon on was the arrival of the car. Within a decade of the publication of the report, there was no longer a horse-generated transport problem. Instead, Dublin was trying to cope with a quite different set of issues, all related to four-wheeled, motorised vehicles rather than four-legged animals. It is very easy to smile indulgently at the planners' lack of foresight, but I am not sure whether their extrapolation from the present, as they saw it, was that different from the mindset that led Bill Gates to underestimate so signally the importance of the Internet in the early years of the World Wide Web.

As Ted Crosbie never underestimated the importance of technology, when, in 1993, I took over as CEO of the *Examiner*, the place looked very strong from the engineering point of view, and rather less strong from the market and financial point of view. Not surprisingly, nobody fought me for the right to take over the running of the family firm at that time. It may not have been a poisoned chalice, but let's just say it was not without its challenges.

Moving into that situation, I had three great advantages. One was that there was only one way the business could go: up. The second was the knowledge that this was a family business with a great sense of its history and its position, both within its immediate catchment area and among the various media in Ireland. The third was an invaluable piece of advice I got from a management-consultant friend. 'When you take over a business,' he said, 'do nothing for the first six months. But if you haven't done a lot by the end of eighteen months, get out.'

For the first six months, I watched and learned. It was difficult not to get in there immediately and do some massive meddling, because it was patently obvious that the company was in dire straits and could fail if radical action was not taken. So patently obvious was this fact that staff at all levels within the organisation recognised such change had to happen. According to much management-consultancy thinking at the moment, this is all you need to effect change throughout a company. Not true, as a couple of professors of Organisational Behaviour and Human Resource Management at the Harvard Business School have pointed out.

'This theory [that, if people get enthusiastic enough, change will happen naturally] gets the change process exactly backward,' the professors say. 'In fact, individual behaviour is powerfully shaped by the organisational roles that people play. The most effective way to change behaviour, therefore, is to put people into a new organisational context, which imposes new roles, responsibilities and relationships on them.'

This, however, was not clear to me at the beginning of my period as CEO. I had the illusory hope that people could change. These days, I am convinced that, while people can be trained to do specific tasks in a different way, it is virtually impossible to get people radically to change their thinking. I took over, indicated the changes the paper needed – and the paper did not change. The people were willing, committed and good at their job, but the product stayed the same.

I do not understand why this surprises business people. It happens outside of business all the time. In 1997, I attended my school's twenty-five-year reunion. It was fascinating. We met in a hotel in Galway for the usual ritual: dinner, drinking, hangover, home. Within minutes of arriving in Galway, we all reverted to type. Faster than you could snap your fingers, there we were, recreated in roles we had filled twenty-five years before. The guys you took the piss out of twenty-five years ago, you were straight into taking the piss out of again now. The guys who hero-worshipped you back then were hero-worshipping you all over again. The guys you didn't like twenty-five years ago, you still didn't like.

The changes the *Examiner* needed were not simple operational changes. They were profound changes in attitude. The attitudes that needed to be changed were not 'bad' attitudes. Nobody was throwing clogs in the machinery or setting out to do the company or the paper any harm. Nonetheless, the attitudes that needed to be changed had been built up over generations, in no small measure because the *Examiner* was a family newspaper. At the core of the problem was the belief among editorial staff that they were producing the paper for the Crosbie family. I was looking for change. 'Up to now, you've prepared the paper for the board,' I would say. 'Now you're going to produce it for the customers out there.'

Intellectually, they agreed with me. In practice, they went on doing what they had previously done, surrounded as they were by the intangible supports – the assumption that this is the way it's always been done, so this is the way it should continue to be done. I was constantly being asked what I thought of a particular edition, and just as constantly saying that it didn't matter what I thought of that or any other edition. Some of the older members of my own family got in on the act out of habit. 'You must have a view,' they said.

Well, as a matter of fact, I mustn't have a view. If I was asked what I was going to do about a particular problem in the print room, I would say I was doing to do nothing about that problem – that the guy in charge of the print room was the person to make the decision about it. If he got it wrong, then we should deal with that, but we shouldn't have someone like me all over his area, when I knew less than he did about what he was doing.

I found myself subject to an unintended form of emotional blackmail as a result of this stance. This emotional blackmail is not unusual in family businesses and stems from the notion that, if you run a business, you should be able to do everything you ask other people to do. You'll hear management quoted along these lines: 'I've never asked any executive to do something I couldn't do myself' or 'My people know, when I instruct them to do something, that I'm au fait with every aspect of what's involved.'

In modern business, this is a self-indulgent, pointless throwback and is insulting to the person who is a specialist in the area involved. CEOs should pick the right people, put them in the right places, give them the right instructions and the appropriate resources and leave them to get on with the job.

At operational levels in most businesses, there is very little value in announcing programmes for change. People can adapt without much hassle to doing their main task slightly differently. It is like the period before gunpowder was invented. In the old days, whichever lord, king or baron was fighting whichever other lord, king or baron did not matter a jot to the peasants. They just got on with planting their potatoes, living their lives and hoping the loony aristocratic factions did not decide to have a battle on the particular bit of farmland in which they had set their spuds.

But then, I have doubts about high-flown programmes of change at most levels. Training can help people strengthen their weaknesses and improve marginally. I simply do not accept claims that training can radically change the way in which people think and react, however. I do not believe that people change in any essential way after they hit their twenties. After that age, they are biologically less open to being influenced by other people. They are 'set', like a jelly, and ready to settle down.

Because of the illusion that enthusiastically announced improvements, supported by training schemes, can change people radically, there is very often a sour period after the first year of a new CEO's arrival, when it becomes obvious that some people are going to have to go. This sourness comes about because of the unreal expectation set up by the 'anybody can change' brigade. The top managers who have intellectually bought in to the planned changes feel very bitter when they find themselves axed, and usually explain it to themselves, in a legitimate attempt to sustain their own self-belief, by suggesting that the new guy was always planning a purge but just didn't have the guts to say so at the beginning. The not-so-new top cat has his – or her – own, contrasting explanation: the old guard were given every opportunity to prove that they were eager to become the new guard, but they wouldn't change, so what choice is there?

The problem is the underlying assumption that radical change results when people have the right attitude. The reality is that what is needed is the right behaviour. Give the new CEO the right behaviour, and it shouldn't matter to him what your attitude is. Give the new CEO the wrong behaviour, and it won't – and indeed can't – matter to him that you have a really good attitude. We pay people for behaviour, not attitude. More to the point, you can spend a lifetime persuading, educating, even seducing people into having the right attitude, and if they still can't adopt the desired behaviour, you may have to remove them, and they, as a result, then rightly feel betrayed.

(By way of illustration, it's worth pointing out that not long ago, in this country, we had a Taoiseach whose *attitude* was that people should live within their means. His *behaviour*, on the other hand, was expensively at variance with this attitude.)

When change takes place at the top, the real casualties are the lieutenants of the previous incumbent. The casualties at the *Examiner* were the people who had got used to the way in which Ted Crosbie, who is now my chairman, operated and could not adapt to the way in which I operated. It was infinitely sad – as it always is – to see people continuing to do with integrity and professionalism what they have been trained to believe is the essence of their job, only to find that, because their environment has changed, that very continuation is giving rise to negative judgements about their future.

The only reason I could sleep at night when I began to move good people from their long-held posts at the paper was because I was able to say, 'It's for the greater good.' In a company context, the happiness of the people has to come after the performance of the company, because if the company is not there, neither are the people – happy or unhappy. I appointed a number of strong people to key positions when I had worked out what was needed at the *Examiner*, and, having appointed them, I let them get on with it. Meetings never last longer than an hour and a half and always reflect our agreed priorities: people and sales. Every decision made within the paper should be informed by working out what a customer would want in that situation.

The *Examiner* in the mid-1990s was a form of battlefield triage. Battlefield triage developed centuries ago, in the great European wars. It happened in the late evenings, when the canons went silent. The army surgeons would go out onto the shadowy, muddied, bloodied field of action to look at the wounded and divide them into three groups. One group was to be left alone because they could not be saved. A second group was to be left alone too; they were the ones who, even though they might not be feeling too

Thomas Edison, the fifth-eldest of ten children, developed the first electric light bulb and the phonograph

Henry Ford, an Irish-American, pioneered the motor car and created the world's largest family business, the Ford Motor Company

Thomas Crosbie, to whom John Francis Maguire left the *Cork Examiner* newspaper, now the *Irish Examiner*

Margaret Heffernan, Ben Dunne Jr's older sister, who has been instrumental in recent years in taking Dunnes Stores upmarket

Billy Higgins

Ben Dunne Jr, who was a significant figure in Dunnes Stores in the 1970s but was effectively prevented from playing an active role in the business in the early 1990s

Billy Higgins

Ben Dunne Sr, who founded Dunnes Stores

Richard Mills

Christy Kelleher, who founded Blarney Woollen Mills. Three of his four sons, all of his three daughters and several of his in-laws are involved in the business

Des Barry

Freda Hayes, Christy Kelleher's daughter, started working for Blarney Woollen Mills at sixteen and now runs her own company

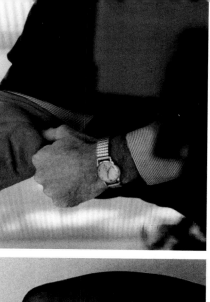

TV personality Bunny Carr, who founded
Carr Communications

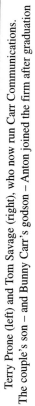

Terry Prone (left) and Tom Savage (right), who now run Carr Communications.
The couple's son – and Bunny Carr's godson – Anton joined the firm after graduation

Maurizio Gucci, the last member of the Gucci family to sit on the company's board

Patrizia Reggiani Martinelli, who had Maurizio, her estranged husband, killed in 1995

Carol Moffett, managing director of Monaghan-based
Moffett Engineering, which was founded
by her father, Cyril Moffett

Stelios Haji-Ioannou, who founded low-cost airline EasyJet after running a
division of his father's shipping empire in Athens

José Raventos, who developed Barcelona-based winemaking company Codorníu's business in the late nineteenth century

Maria Raventós, chairman of Codorníu. She is descended from Jaime Codorníu, who founded the firm in 1551

good, were nonetheless going to be OK even if they received no medical help. Then, there was the third category. This group consisted of those that could survive if major investment of surgical skill and attention was lavished on them, and if they had a passion to survive. It is much the same in any business where massive change has to be achieved against a tight deadline: it is triage time.

The first group to be identified consists of the people who cannot change and cannot survive within the company. The second group consists of those who will adapt even if you more or less leave them alone. The third group is made up of individuals who can change, survive, develop and grow – if you get them into the right position. (This may well be a quite different position to the one they have most recently occupied. Every now and then, a radical improvement in the performance of a staff member is attributed to the charismatic qualities of a new boss, when what has in fact happened is that the employee has been shifted from a position to which they were never suited to a position that fits them like a glove.)

In most organisations, when someone is underperforming, the assumption at management level is either that the underperformer needs a good rollocking or that they need more training, when what they may in fact need is a change of position. The underperformer is a round peg in a square hole. Get them into a square hole and their productivity goes through the roof. This sounds obvious, but more orthodox management thinking is that anybody can be retrained to cope with a new scenario. I don't believe this is the case. I don't think, for example, that you can take the entire cast of *Cats*, train them in free verse and expect them – one and all – to perform well in *Hamlet*.

In any organisation, massive change against a deadline requires people at the top to do triage. But doing this has two extra attendant difficulties in a family business. The first of these is that those who must go find the experience particularly cruel, because they had a real sense of belonging to the family, and now a new generation of that family is 'rejecting' them.

The second great difficulty is that family businesses, unlike shareholder-owned ones, rarely present a completely new set of options to the incoming CEO. In many cases, the old CEO maintains an office on the premises, 'just to keep an eye on things'. The older generation never say, 'just to keep an eye on you', but that is what they mean. Either way, a physical personification of the old ways is ever-present, and the very presence of the old boss can unintentionally subvert what the new boss is trying to achieve.

For a couple of years at the *Examiner*, things were very tough, especially for good people whose ways would not allow them to contribute to the future of the paper. By 1995, however, we had a coherent team pulling together. We had sales-oriented editors, great systems, good technology and a couple of good strategic alliances. But we had a unique geographic situation. More than a third of the population of Ireland lives in Dublin. All daily media, with the exception of our own papers, emanate from the capital.

That gave us an advantage and a problem. We could batten down the hatches, concentrate on Cork and stay put. Nobody wanted to do that. It meant we would have been standing still – a frank impossibility in a business like newspapers, where you are either moving forward or dead in the water. Another possible avenue was to launch a Sunday newspaper. This option carried with it the dread possibility that, if it failed, it might take the daily papers with it.

The third choice was to make the paper a serious alternative to the other nationals and sell it outside Cork. If we wanted to do that, we would face an immediate problem: we would need to have people in Cavan or Clonmel, Galway or Dublin pick up the newspaper because something about its front page attracted them to it. But they were never going to do that if the word 'Cork' was sitting smack in the middle of the title. As long as that was there, potential readers would never see the paper as a real alternative to their usual purchase. (Remember that their usual paper was not called the *Dublin Times* or the *Dublin Independent*.)

So, after 155 years we decided to take the first step in a two-step operation. We decided to take the word 'Cork' out of the title. At the back of our minds, we had the plan to rename the paper, at some time in the future, the *Irish Examiner*, but first we needed to see whether there would be a major hostile reaction within our own bailiwick to the removal of the name of the location from the title. There was no hostile reaction at all. Later research showed that regular readers were, in fact, delighted that, as they saw it, 'their' paper had staked its claim to the national ground to which it was entitled.

As part of claiming that national status, we had to reach markets like Dublin. But we also knew that, if we wanted to reach markets like Dublin, we had to produce the bulk of our papers earlier than we would do if they were to continue to sell only in Cork. So we decided to bring out the paper earlier. We then began to produce three different editions for different parts of the country.

The newspaper's finances came back into the black. Reinforcement for what we were doing came from sales, from advertising, from readers, from our own staff and from our profit figures.

Much the same had happened with our evening paper, the *Echo*. That paper had for some time suffered from falling circulation and advertising. In fact, at one point, we had come within 1,000 copies of the point at which the *Echo* would have become a liability rather than an asset. It was turned around and within two years had become the only evening newspaper in the whole of Ireland and Britain with a rising circulation. Since then, the *Echo* has improved further, with a special edition being produced for Limerick.

7
—

THE SUCCESSION PROBLEM

Allow me to introduce you to David Goldstein. David is an old friend of mine who, when I first met him, owned and ran a Chicago-based clothing company which sells its products all over the world. David is Jewish and has strong family values.

Six or seven years ago, the two of us spoke about what he was going to do with his company. He was, at that time, almost sixty. He had three sons, and he told me he was going to divide the company up equally between the three of them.

'You're out of your mind,' I told him. 'Pick out the one who's best suited to running the business and give it to him, or sell the whole thing off and divide the money between them.'

He went his own way, as we both knew he would. A year or two later, when I met him again, I found him in his office, poring over architects' plans.

'David, what are the plans for?' I asked him.

'I'm trying to solve the problem of having three offices – one for each of my boys.'

'What's the problem?'

'They have to be of equal size because the two of them are at odds about the size – the relative size – of the offices each of them has right now.'

'David?'

'Mmm?'

'I hate to say this to you, but I told you so.'

'Alan?'

'Mmm?'

'I hate to say this to you, but I love my sons more than my business.'

If you equate love for your kids with love of your business, you end up with the worst of all possible options on both sides. You stop making the right business decisions. You simply cannot be completely fair to a business and at the same time completely fair to all members of the family: you have to pick one of the family, if there is one who is manifestly best suited to run the business. In short, you have to show tough love.

Of course, making that choice can be easier than making it stick, as I found out when I met a man at a business lunch on this topic in London. This man had just left his teaching job, because an old bachelor uncle of his had left him the business the uncle had set up decades earlier. The uncle had left the business to him lock, stock and barrel. It was a good business, well cared for, very much a going concern, up to its armpits in goodwill – and all his.

On the other hand, this man's demeanour did not bespeak delight. In fact, he looked pretty depressed. The reason was that his own brothers and sisters had decided, as soon as they found out about his good fortune, that his visits to his old uncle during his summer holidays were part of a wicked plot. The visits were a way of sucking up to the uncle in order to get the old man to leave his business to the young teacher when the businessman died. The brothers and sisters decided that each of them was just as entitled as the young teacher was to the company and that they would go to court to vindicate their sense of entitlement.

They should never have had that sense of entitlement in the first place. Their uncle had quite rightly picked out one of them to give the firm to. He knew the power of one and had the wit to realise that only one of his nephews and nieces had the wherewithal to pick up and run the business he had created.

In due course, the former teacher came to a settlement with his brothers and sisters which involved him giving each of them some money. It was a good way of getting them off his back. The worst possible option would have been to have had him as CEO and several of them as shareholders, because the shareholders appoint the board and the board controls the CEO. Thus, when a business founder who is also a father or mother decides that they will play it really smart in the succession stakes by not dividing everything evenly but instead leaving one of the family as chief executive and ensuring that the rest of the clan are simply shareholders, they are often not being smart at all but are in fact ensuring that the chief executive is crippled from the beginning. This is what seems to have happened not once, but twice, in the case of Blarney Woollen Mills.

One of the problems inherent in giving advice to parents about choosing one successor rather than deciding that all of their children should run the family business is that parents are notoriously poor judges of the capacities of their children. Any one of us can think of some friend who believes his son or daughter is possessed of wonderful talent, amiability and intelligence, even though it is perfectly plain to any outsider that the kid is a complete waste of space. Contrariwise, any of us can think of a friend who has written off her son as unreliable, unlikeable and in every way a disappointment, whereas to people outside the family, he seems to be stuffed full of potential and even charm.

Our judgement, when applied to our own family, tends to be questionable, but every now and then a family-business founder or CEO applies his judgement to the next generation, decides one of them can eventually make it as the top dog and starts grooming them for that position. As the current CEO is at the top of a family business, however, not all of the rules apply to him – including the rule about retiring at sixty-five.

So at seventy, the father may still be in place. Or at seventy-five. There are numerous examples of family businesses ostensibly being run by the next generation, whereas, in fact, a founder long past the traditional retirement age is holding on to the reins. In the past, the plight of ageing single men waiting for their fathers to hand over the family farm so that they could court, marry and begin their 'real adult life' was a recurrent theme of plays in the Abbey Theatre in Dublin. These days, in a scatter of industrial sectors and in every county in Ireland, there are tragedies being played out along much the same lines every day. In such cases, one generation uses the excuse that the next generation needs just a bit more time and supervision before finally taking over the business the parent claims to be willing to hand on. That excuse prevents the parent from having to retire and leave the running of the business to someone else.

I'm not ageist, but not everybody is as functional at seventy-five as they were at fifty-five. But of course, if the person in question is a family member – particularly a family member who set up or radically enlarged the family business – belling the cat can be difficult, and nobody may have the courage to tell Uncle Wally to leave the board. That is one of the key issues with families: they are often ridiculously soft-hearted when it comes to making business decisions involving relatives but unspeakably hard-hearted when relationships break down – and relationships are most likely to break down at the time of succession. In that regard, running a family business is very much like flying a plane. There is not much danger to anybody when the plane is in the third hour of a transatlantic journey, but at take-off and landing the craft is much more vulnerable to an accident. The point of succession is very like landing and taking off again. It presents a radically greater threat of danger than is posed by any of the other periods in the history of the company.

The older generation can be either helpful or unhelpful in this kind of situation. They will be unhelpful if they send mixed signals: on the one hand indicating that they would really love to be out of the business and improving their golf swing or taking long cruises in the tropics, and on the other hand maintaining an office on the premises and keeping their little finger in every corporate pie. The need to believe oneself to be indispensable leads to stupid and selfish behaviour. If you are important in your family business and genuinely believe that nobody in the next generation is going to come near you when it comes to ability to manage the business, then tell them so and give them a bundle of money and a ticket to Outer Mongolia, but don't keep them hanging on in the front office waiting for you to be inspired by some commercial God reaching down out of the clouds with tablets of stone that say, 'Junior is grown up enough now, retire and let him at it.'

Second-generation family-business leaders, in my experience, are just as, if not more, tenacious than actual founders when it comes to hanging on to the business rather than letting go of it and handing it on to the third generation. This may be a result of not being a founder. There may be an unspoken, unacknowledged pressure on the second generation to prove to onlookers that they put some kind of personal stamp on the business, even if they did not actually set it up.

In that regard, I believe the Crosbies have a worthwhile approach. They talk of the business being 'on loan' to them, and, as the fifth-generation scion, I am particularly conscious of it being a short-term loan I would rather pay back before it gets recalled. From the moment I took over, I had a mental deadline on how long I would stay as CEO, and I think many people in my kind of situation would not be badly served by the system which now applies to the secretary-generals at the top of government departments. These officials are much better paid than the old department secretaries were, but they operate on a seven-year contract which does not have renewal built into it. The turnover of secretary-generals according to this seven-year cycle is undoubtedly good for the department involved and – assuming the man or woman at the top is not the sort of person who wants to get the plum job and then coast forever after – is probably very good for the secretary-general too.

I will stop being CEO of Examiner Publications while still relatively young, first of all because I think I need to, and secondly because I think it will be good for the business for someone else to take over. When business friends ask, 'Why don't you stay on until one of your kids is old enough to take over?' my answer is, 'Who knows whether any of my kids would want to take over – or be suitable to take over? The family does not have a divine right to run the business.'

This creates a curious, two-way pressure. Quite often, the older family member is reluctant to hand over the reins of management to a non-family member because of a vague dynastic feeling that one of his or her own kids should eventually run the business. In staying on with that purpose in mind, the older family member may damage the business. The new broom who comes in and changes everything can find that, five or six years later, everything has changed except the broom itself. It is dangerously tempting to keep things ticking over until the next generation is ready – dangerous because hanging on is addictive. You can get to like it, so that when the next generation is ready, you are not. But it is dangerous, too, in that a perhaps unspoken assumption builds up in the family that one or more of the next generation should want to go into the family business and perhaps even owes it to mum or dad to do so because their parents kept the seat warm for them.

Vagueness about how long a family CEO should run the company belongs to the past. These days, terms should be set from the beginning. The attrition which means that more family businesses move out of family ownership with every passing generation could be lessened if families had some kind of informal agreement as to how long each CEO would be allowed to hold the top job. Indeed, some business consultants maintain that a formal constitution should be agreed within the family to obviate the grief and disruption which too often develops in areas of imprecision.

Similarly, the seminal figures in family businesses should be wary of using their wills in a self-serving way. I suppose it's only natural that, if you have built a business from nothing and have the thing singing along, making money in bucketfuls, you would consider it your entitlement to have a bit of fun – a bit of self-expression in the will you write. Why not heavily reward the children or grandchildren or nephews and nieces you think are the good ones and ignore those you dislike or find extremely boring?

Any business person making out their will this year should keep one consideration at the back of their mind: you might die. People who are relatively young when they make their wills never for a moment imagine that they may die soon, and so the will becomes a matter of self-expression rather than a serious issue which might have lethal consequences for the family business. It is worthwhile not only to consider the possibility of actually dying but also to tell family members the content of your will so that they are not living in cloud-cuckoo-land.

The old-fashioned view of a will as a matter of self-expression rather than of realistic family-business planning seems to have been the way Gianni Versace thought when he was deciding who would inherit the millions from the business he had created from his own design genius and to which his brother and sister had both made enormous personal commitments. Versace did not know that his life was going to be cut short by an obsessed murderer. He may even have thought of his will as little more than a holding statement, to be amended as he got older. The will, drawn up ten months before Versace was killed, gave a 50 per cent share in his business to his favourite niece, Allegra. While he was still alive, Versace had divided the other half of the company – which the previous year had had a turnover of £600 million – between his brother Santo and his sister Donatella.

Versace's will, which singled out Donatella's daughter for an inheritance of 50 per cent, means that, in the short to medium term, Donatella, who is widely regarded as her brother's creative heir, has 70 per cent of the voting shares. As if that was not hard enough for her brother Santo to take, the will made it plain that Gianni had little or no time for Santo's children: they were completely excluded from it, although Allegra's younger brother Daniel got Gianni's art collection, which includes a Picasso or two.

Financial commentators at Italy's *La Repubblica* newspaper were quick to point out that, unless Santo had the skin of a rhino, the shape of the will must be offensive to him. 'I wouldn't be at all surprised if the two major family interests now decided to go their own ways,' said one of those commentators. 'This testament presents a host of potential problems.'

Versace could not have anticipated those problems, nor their happening just as the company he had created was preparing to float on Wall Street. But if, when he sat down to draw up his will, he had considered the health and future of his business rather than the pleasure of rewarding family members he favoured, he could have ensured that the surname he made instantly recognisable worldwide would continue into the next century, whereas now, that is far from guaranteed.

Older-generation family-business members should look at their own retirement, and at their will, with the interests of the business very much in mind. They should also look at the business's present phase of development, as they approach pre-retirement age. Many businesses, particularly in new areas, are created by highly innovative, risk-addicted entrepreneurs – pioneers going into unmapped territory and uncharted waters, hunting down new markets. By the time the founder is ready to think about moving on, the shape of the CEO's role may have been altered by the changing requirements of the business. In simple terms, the business may no longer require a risk-taking, swashbuckling pioneer, but a consolidator.

If the founder projects his or her own personality as essential to the business's future and seeks out among their offspring a carbon copy of themselves, they may be doing their business – and the second-generation individual who is selected – enormous damage. The business founder who discovers that one of their children has obvious entre-preneurial flair may be best advised to invest in that flair – but not necessarily by pulling the younger entrepreneur into the family business.

That is what Stelios Haji-Ioannou's father did when, in his twenties, Stelios got bored of running a divison of his parent's shipping empire in Athens. The father gave him £5 million and told him to go and make a name for himself. Stelios travelled, looked at various businesses and settled on one that was not very different from his father's. He had seen budget airlines making a lot of money in the United States and had become a fan of Richard Branson and his Virgin operation. He therefore decided to create a low-cost airline called EasyJet. Four years after he set it up, the airline had twenty routes, a hundred flights a day, 1,000 staff, five million customers a year and an estimated market value of £120 million.

Not bad for a thirty-two-year-old. But what is most interesting about the success of EasyJet is that it was achieved by virtue of the fact that the young Greek voluntarily cut away all the comforts to which he could so easily have become addicted when he was working for his father. Back then, he had had luxurious desks and two secretaries. Now, he doesn't even have an office: he very occasionally sits at a desk in the middle of a large, open-plan barn at Luton Airport. Money is not spent on the appearance of the place, nor on comforts for the chief executive, because even though the business is making profits, those profits are being ploughed into more important purchases, like aeroplanes. At the moment, he is buying a new plane every month, on average. Stelios has numerous big plans for EasyJet and has already struck fear into the hearts of several much longer established, national brand airlines. Fair dues to him.

But fair dues also to his father, who spotted in the younger man the signs of entrepreneurship. The father had the wit to let his son go and to fund him to set up another business, instead of forcing him to stay in a role which, at this point, probably requires a quite different mindset and attitude. The shipping empire may now require a consolidator rather than an adventurer, but it takes a clever man to spot the difference and to give the adventurer son carte blanche to explore and experiment, rather than straitjacketing him into a post within the family business where his natural talents could find little outlet and his deficits would inevitably come to the fore.

Another company which has gone to considerable trouble not only to ensure the long-term survival of its operations within family hands but also to buttress family solidarity is Johnson Wax, the US-based furniture-polish makers. Johnson Wax was set up 113 years ago and is now worth $5 billion. The current chairman, Samuel Curtis Johnson, who is in his seventies, was bothered, in his middle years, by incidents in corporate history which suggested that keeping the business in the family while ensuring that it remained successful was not a matter of easy wishful thinking. He began to read everything he could lay his hands on about family enterprises and turned himself into something of an expert on the factors that bring down such businesses. He began to look at three of his four children very carefully, giving them opportunities within the corporation in areas he believed suited their different personalities and sets of skills.

As time went on, the next generation came to some surprising conclusions. For example, one of Johnson's daughters didn't want to run any aspect of Johnson Wax. She was a mother of four and wanted to work part-time in one of the corporation's divisions. Three of her siblings, however, emerged as having both the capacity and the interest to be CEOs. Their father looked at this and – in constant discussion with them – came to a consensus decision that three CEOs was too many for a single entity. On the other hand, if Johnson Wax were to be broken down into some of its component parts, each of the three could head up those parts. It was an unusual plan and needed a great deal of teasing out before it could be finalised to the agreement of all parties – but finalised it was, last year.

Breaking a huge conglomerate into three unequal parts is a fairly radical step to take in order to avoid family conflict, but the chairman and his children believe it to have been an appropriate step. 'One thing I know about brothers working for brothers,' the chairman says, 'is that it always has the potential for disruption.'

At various points in its history, the corporation went through major disruption, including a situation where a Johnson in the main line of succession died without leaving a will – a problem that took ten years to solve and left bitter traces in many family relationships thereafter. Nonetheless, the company had lasted to the fifth generation before the innovative break-up scheme was implemented, in 1999. The fact that the company survived under family control to that point is extraordinary.

When we look at the statistics of family businesses, it is very easy to be seduced by the simplicity of some of the numbers. According to the small and medium enterprises development centre at Manchester Business School, for example, 'the family-business economy represents 85 per cent of all enterprises across the EU.' Meanwhile, the Netherlands Business School reports that '47 per cent of Dutch companies with a hundred or more employees are family businesses, and 83 per cent of all businesses in the Netherlands are family-owned.' In addition, those family businesses account for 46 per cent of jobs in the Netherlands and 54 per cent of the country's gross domestic product.

On the other hand, Joseph Astrachan, a professor of Family Business at Kennesaw University in Georgia, says a family business has only a one in fifty chance of surviving in family hands to the fifth generation. That statistic makes sense of the effort the Johnson Wax people have put into getting things right. They have set up family councils to meet and resolve sources of conflict, and in the planning of the careers of the three who are now to become CEO, not only were periods outside the family business encouraged for those who at first did not see themselves joining the dynasty, but great care was taken to ensure that none of the siblings directly reported to another sibling during their industrially formative years.

It is highly significant – and will probably give pause to many other large-scale family businesses – that the head of such a large corporation would give such time and thought, over a period of three decades, to the possibility of maintaining his corporation in family hands while not allowing family participation to cause friction between brothers and sisters. The penny seems to be dropping: family businesses do not successfully remain in the family if shareholdings and management positions are dished out promiscuously to all members of the next generation in a way that makes the present generation feel good.

These days, later generations are more choosy about their career options than they were in the past. In earlier times, founders could more readily assume that their children would want to go into the business – and would be suited to it. Young people had fewer options and were more easily pressured by parents. But nowadays young people are being brought up to do their own thing and go their own way. So the deceptively easy option of bringing them all into the family business is – fortunately – less attractive.

Nonetheless, most families, to this day, tend to look to the family first when they address the issue of who will succeed to the family firm. The majority of families, when they express the hope that 'the business will stay in the family', are not referring solely to the ownership of the business. They are usually also expressing the hope that the business will continue to be run by the family. In that context, my own family firm is an exception. We know for certain that the next chief executive of Examiner Publications is not going to be a Crosbie. That is now accepted by everybody in the family; acceptance of this was helped by the fact that the move breaks no great family tradition.

The continuity of the role of chief executive has not been there for five generations, because the position of chief executive has been there for only two generations. Ted Crosbie, my predecessor, was actually the first CEO of the company. The chairman always ran the business before that, and his roles was much more loosely defined than the CEO's is now.

One reason for me to continue running the business – that there is no other family member to do it – would be the wrong justification for me to carry on as the boss. Taking such a course of action would be to assume that nobody in the whole wide world other than a Crosbie is capable of running the business. This is poppycock.

If any one of my children is capable of running the business – and wants to do so – then they have a pretty good chance of making it, because whoever is Examiner Publications' CEO in the future will have a contract rather than life tenure. Anyone who is running the business – including me, right now – will have a defined contract. One of the reasons I am setting the precedent that nobody – be they a Crosbie or not – should be chief executive for life is to generate constant change so that there are always positions and people available.

It is important to remember that 'succession' has a substantially different meaning these days from the meaning it had in the past. Previously, a managing director might work until sixty-five or seventy and then hand over to the next generation, who, in turn, might run the company for twenty, thirty or forty years. It is fairly widely agreed that leaving one person in a top management role for that length of time is rarely good for either the company or the individual. The periods of time spent at managing-director level are shorter. There are people who want to spend five or six years running a business and then move on to something else. So even if a family business takes on an outsider as chief executive, this should not be seen, either inside or outside the family, as meaning that the firm will always be run by a non-family member. Whoever wants to compete for the role at the top of a family-owned business – be they a family member or not – should find their chance coming up in time.

Moreover, family and non-family members should have an equal chance of getting the top post. Families should learn to keep the lines clear: there is a huge difference between ownership and management. Just because you own something does not mean you are the best person to manage it.

Indeed, I would maintain that educating the family on the difference between equity and executive role and that kind of thing should be done as early as humanly possible, because of the grief caused when family members become convinced that shareholding should – or does – imply that they should take a hands-on interest in the governance of the business.

Being chief executive in a family business in so many families is a poisoned chalice, If you're in a situation where, whether you go right or go left or go forward, you're wrong every time, you can't operate. You're in an impossible situation. The only people who whacked it long ago were the Japanese, with their Shogun-type family businesses, where they appointed one member.

Indeed, I have already said that our ancestors, with their primogeniture system of inheritance, had something going for them. It may not have been fair that the eldest son inherited the family business, but, on the other hand, at least only one person inherited. This at least meant that family businesses could not be fragmented by the multiple claimants that became typical once inheritance law changed and owners of businesses became more committed to fairness and equity.

There is much more to managing the succession issue than dividing the spoils evenly. In fact, I would go further: dividing the spoils evenly is probably the single worst thing the head of any generation within a family business can do.

8

―

WATCHING OUT FOR POTENTIAL

This may be a strange point at which to draw back and start looking at definitions, but one of the oddities of family businesses is that nobody is entirely sure what constitutes such a business. It is easy enough if you have a husband and wife who set up an operation, own it, run it and eventually involve their children in it. But what if the operation is set up by one man, then later run by a husband-and-wife team unrelated by blood to the founder, as is the case with Carr Communications in Dublin.

The founder of Carr Communications was TV personality Bunny Carr. Since the 1980s, the firm has been run by Terry Prone and Tom Savage, each of whom has a substantial shareholding in it. Their son – and the founder's godson – Anton joined the company after graduation. But does that make the firm a family business?

'Technically, it probably isn't a family business,' says Managing Director Terry Prone. 'We have five shareholders and seven directors, and no one family owns even close to 50 per cent of the business. Yet we tend to nod when people talk of it as a family business, because I suppose the lives of Bunny, Tom and me have been so intertwined, and our thinking runs along such parallel lines, it *feels* like a family.'

That company would be at one end of a continuum, at

the other end of which is the firm that is completely owned by one family. Between those two extremes, a plethora of other configurations exist. In some of the textbooks I have examined, the definition of the amount of equity a family must have in order for their enterprise to be called a family business ranges between 60 per cent and 100 per cent. In others, majority shareholding is all that is required. One definition even suggested that the ownership of any percentage of the stock would do, provided the family could determine the outcome of any issue that is brought to a shareholder vote.

One authority on the subject, Reginald A. Litz, has proposed three variations on what might define a family business:

- A business firm may be considered a family business to the extent that its ownership and management are concentrated within a family.
- A business firm may be considered a family business to the extent that its members strive to achieve, maintain and/or increase intra-organisational family-based relatedness.
- A business firm may be considered a family business to the extent that its ownership and management are concentrated within a family unit and to the extent that its members strive to achieve, maintain and/or increase intra-organisational family-based relatedness.

Now it might be simpler to suggest that, if it quacks like a family business and thinks of itself as a family business, there is a very good chance it *is* a family business. However,

as family businesses become global operations, the definitions begin to seem more important.

There is, for example, the issue of funding for massive
expansion. A family may decide to seek a stock-exchange
listing in order to obtain the equity funding they need for
planned growth. Inevitably, this means giving away some
measure of their control over their own company, but —
according to some observers — such loss of control can be
more than compensated for by the globalisation, scale and
professionalism that comes into the business as a direct
result of this listing.

Whereas some family businesses, like Hermés in France,
find that going for a stock-market listing forces them
radically to improve their operation, too many family
businesses stumble at the point of transition from first to
second generation because no such external pressure exists.
The company, under its founder, has been doing very well.
Typically, it has been doing the same thing very well for
a considerable length of time, and the founder assumes it
will continue to do very well for a considerable period in
the future. Also typically, the founder believes he or she
will do the right thing by their family if they split the
business and, just as importantly, will split control of the
business evenly between all of their children.

The founder does this without ever looking at the
differing potential of their children, mainly because few
parents have the capacity to stand back and assess which
of their children are stayers and which are 'neophiliacs'.
Neophiliacs are addicted to what is new. They try one sport
after another and end up never mastering any one of them.
It is a characteristic that is easy to spot even in a child as
young as seven or eight. The stayer, on the other hand, may

be utterly defeated – trounced, even – on their first outing onto a football field or into a swimming race, yet they will doggedly practice until they get a handle on the sport.

Another trait that is easy to distinguish early on is the need for instant gratification. Some children can postpone eating a sweet for a long time; others need to unwrap it and have at it right away. Someone setting out to run a family business usually needs the capacity to postpone gratification.

If you are running a family business and you want your children to play a part in the business, think again. Or rather, look again. Look at your children from the time they are very small, and you will spot, at quite an early stage, whether they will be suited or spavined by joining the family business. When I say 'quite early', I mean as early as eleven. Maybe as early as nine. Watch them with their peers. Watch for whether they are leaders or not. Watch for whether they have staying power or give up easily. The signs are obvious. Your child will say, 'I'm going to try playing soccer', and then, half an hour later, will announce that, 'I'm no good at soccer. I want to play something else.'

I am conscious that it sounds unpaternal and very harsh for people running the family business to start looking at their children in a judgemental way. Maybe so, but this approach is a great deal kinder, in the long run, than the attack of sentimentality that strikes the many business people who look at their families and say 'This is all for you. I did this all for you.' Then they say, 'Equity demands that all four of my children get equal shares' (or however many children they have). They divide up the shares, give jobs to all of their children, and wait for the line that runs,

'And they all lived happily ever after.' In fact, the line is much more likely to read, 'And at this point, all hell broke loose.'

Hell almost invariably follows brainless sentimentality – the sort of brainless sentimentality family-business operators should not show. Here's the deal. You own and run a family business. You have, say, five kids. You've reared your family and you've given your family a level of living they've come to expect. You take that business and divide it among five. Let's say three of them get married. A business that provided a good living for you and your family now effectively – including your spouse in the equation – has to support nine individuals plus their offspring. And the original four still expect the same standard of living. So you've multiplied what must be taken out of the business by five or more.

The sums don't add up – and the arithmetic is based on some daft concept of equity. Equity for whom? The family or the business? You have to make a choice. If you choose family, you might as well say, 'to hell with the business'. Sooner or later, the situation is as stark as that. If you divide the shares evenly among your kids and divide responsibility for how the company is run in the same way, you sow the seeds of later disaster. In setting out to be fair to a family, the founder or owner often in fact does them a huge disservice by effectively setting it up for internal conflict.

One of the problems with bringing family members into the running of the business, even when they seem to have the talent for it or interest in it, lies in the very nature of the family itself. Familiarity breeds contempt. You can see it in many families. How they talk about each other. They have no respect for each other. What you need in a business is people who always focus on the good points and try to work on them. Any one of my managers might be weak at one thing but fantastic at other things – that overall picture. That's what you do in a normal business, and you overlook the things that drive you mad sometimes because the other things are too good. But in a family, it's, 'I'm your brother so I know all your weaknesses.' There's a lack of respect for the individual's abilities, and they harp on the negative. I don't know why. And it's easy to find the negative.'

Bearing all these caveats in mind, if there are a couple of family members who can genuinely handle the next phase of the family business and want to be involved in it, they should of course be brought on board. I would like to see more of my family in my own business, for example. But they should be groomed, trained and selected for posts within the company based on skill and aptitude, not on mere presence and blood relationship. The *Washington Post* has done this beautifully: most of the second generation are not involved in running the paper; some of them are writers, but only one of them has succeeded his mother in the top job.

Looking at the second or third generation in a spirit of unthinking optimism – so that you believe all of them will be making a good living from the business – means your chances of building profits year by year are somewhere between slim and non-existent. It also means that you miss potential elsewhere within your business. John Francis Maguire, the founder of the *Cork Examiner*, did his business a great favour when he spotted the talents of a non-family member named Thomas Crosbie. Many family businesses miss out on huge staff potential because their focus on developing people from within the family makes them myopic about non-family talent, even when that talent is under their nose. These days, when 'recruit' and 'retain' are the watchwords in virtually all businesses, no enterprise can afford to make this mistake.

Talent-spotting management watches and listens – and not just at recruitment interviews, but at production or project meetings. It is very easy, when you stay in touch with the processes by which your business lives, to spot the people with potential. They are the ones who never say, 'It'll do' or, 'That's not my area'. Rather, they are the ones who look at any problem in a slightly offbeat way; the ones who, when you point out that something they have done is wrong, do not start emitting a fog of self-defence but, instead, immediately acknowledge the cock-up and seek help in fixing it. They are never the ones coming behind everybody's back to tell tales to management, but they very definitely are the ones who, when their team does a good job, make sure management knows about each and every member of the team who contributed to it.

In addition to listening to your own people, a key way to identify talent – whether among family members of staff or among non-family staffers – is to remain au fait with training and development. I have not given either of those words a capital letter, because that might imply that you have a separate department devoted to them, and if you're running a small to medium-size business, the chances are that you will not have such a department. The absence of a training-and-development department should not mean, however, that there is no investment on your company's part in the skills and competences of the people who work for you. If there is no such investment, you will lose the best of your people. Training is one of the best untaxable perks for staff these days.

Above all, make sure members of your staff know you are serious when you talk about developing and promoting them. There is, inevitably, doubt in the minds of people working in family businesses about the reality of management claims that there is no limit to how high a non-family member can rise in the company. Yeah, right, staff members think. Like they're not going to fast-track the boss's son? Or the boss's daughter? Tell us another one.

Because of such cynicism, when you run a family business, you have to make it inescapably clear that you mean what you say when you claim that potential, rather than blood relationship, is what counts in the promotion stakes. Saying it early and often helps, but making it real by selecting and promoting talented outsiders is the ultimate proof.

9

THE BOARD GAME

When you look at the board of directors in many family firms, your blood begins to run lukewarm, if not actually cold. 'In the first ten years of our business,' the financial controller of a household-name family business told me, 'We never, *ever* managed to have a board meeting. We tried a number of times, but our two top people were married to each other at the time, and whereas they could work together on a daily basis without much problem, something about the formality of a board meeting brought out the absolute worst in both of them, and they disagreed before the minutes were read. It was so embarrassing for the rest of us, we stopped pushing for board meetings. But of course, that meant that there was really no strategic planning of any kind going on, and in addition, areas of the company business began to be shapeless and un-controlled.'

Eventually, that company's top executives developed a number of protocols for the way in which board members should behave at meetings but, to this day, I would regard that company's board – and the firm's use of it – as one of the profound weaknesses in their business.

Another troubled family business has a board of directors made up entirely of family members. That, in the chief executive's view, is a major error. 'Our parents created the business, and I was working here from very early on,' he says. 'Then they died within a year of each other, and suddenly every family member wanted on to the board. As if that wasn't bad enough, they all decided that the chairman should be the one who knew least about the business, who lives on the other side of the country and who is an academic. I think they felt that, since I had never gone to university, it would give more class to the business if a near-professor was chairman. I couldn't believe, at the first meeting, his lack of skills. I thought that would be one thing he would have, as a result of his education – but no. Where he should be holding the balance, instead he's expressing opinions all the time; patronising me all the time. He basically wouldn't know how to do a day's work. His whole contribution is fighting, fighting, fighting, and wanting studies done on this, that and the other, and the weird thing is that his guff is more impressive to my brothers and sisters than the figures I'm delivering. He suggested at the last meeting that we should really have a rota of CEOs. One of us would do it for every two years. Can you imagine?'

Because so many family firms start from the grinding hard work of one or more clan members, this kind of company tends to be much slower in coming to acknowledge the need for formal corporate governance than, say, a company set up by investors or one resulting from a split-off from a larger business. The tradition in family businesses is hands-on, so there is no immediate value for the operators in the concept of a formal board of directors.

If your business is a tiny corner shop providing a 'lifestyle' career for one or perhaps two people, this thinking makes sense. If, however, you plan expansion, development and a long-term future in which the business supports not only one or two employees but also a great many people outside of the family itself – and generates substantial profits into the bargain – then you need to have not only a board of directors on paper but a real board of directors which is taken seriously by those who are running the company.

Directing a company is quite different from being involved in the everyday running of the same company. Directing a business means making strategic decisions, looking at long-range possibilities and deciding on the allocation of major resources, whether they be financial – money going into new plant or equipment – or human.

Many business founders convince themselves that, because they are so in touch with the day-to-day realities of their market, they have a better strategic sense than any outsider is likely to have. Not so. Bill Gates is no slouch when it comes to running Microsoft. He has built up his personal wealth out of that corporation so that he is worth more than the whole of the Irish economy. But when the Internet came along, he initially underestimated its significance.

Ask the chief executive of any family business about the board of that business, and not only does their answer tell you a great deal about where their business is at the moment, where it came from and where it is likely to go to, but even the quality of the pause before the answer comes will tell you something about the enterprise.

- A slightly distracted hesitation can indicate that the chief executive never pays a blind bit of attention to the board, regarding it the way our grandparents viewed the good china: as being something between a decoration and a personal validation. I have one, I keep it clean and polished and I make sure nobody ever gets the idea that it has any real, day-to-day function to fulfil or contribution to make.

- When the CEO's lips press hard against each other and he or she breathes in deeply through the nose, the chances are that the board is more powerful than the CEO would wish – and much more likely to intervene on a daily basis.

- Eyes rolling to heaven and a finger pointed at your tape recorder to get you to stop it invariably means that the CEO is driven demented by their board and – as frequently happens, nationally and internationally – is likely to end up facing some or all of its members in a courtroom.

- Now and then, a CEO will shrug. This will be not a negative shrug but a neutral-to-positive shrug, indicating the chief executive's view that, in much the same way as it has to have an audit, a company has to have a board of directors, so let's live with it and get the best we can out of it.

Only very occasionally do you come across a family-business board of directors that is greatly valued by the CEO and seen throughout the company as a major contributor to the firm's profitability and identity. I suspect this is because of the way most family businesses are set up. They start, as our earlier chapters have established, when a bright, driven opportunist sees a market gap and seeks to exploit it. Business founders tend to be all-or-nothing people: competent in a range of skills, committed heart and soul to the business and often gifted with vision based on insight and something close to prophecy. The success of the business, based on those traits, is a powerful, indeed constant, reinforcement of these characteristics.

Successful founder CEOs gain more and more confidence in their ability to spot market trends and their capacity to make the right decisions. They rarely wake up in the middle of the night with a metaphorical light bulb flashing above their heads, thinking, 'Hey, you know what I need? I really need a good board of directors.' Of course, when they decide to make the move beyond being sole traders, they may set up a small, nominal board – never going beyond the statutory two members – because the rules say they must. But the classic innovative entrepreneur rarely sees the need for a balanced, multifaceted board of directors. Dominic Ellickson would be a case in point.

Ellickson qualified as an electrical engineer in England in 1960, came back to Ireland and worked for several Irish companies, including ABB, the Waterford firm known at the time as ACEC. His first start-up, in partnership with his wife, Noeleen, was Ellickson Engineering in Waterford, established in 1967. 'I got fed up taking orders,' he remembers. 'We decided when I was thirty and Noeleen had had our first two babies that we'd have a go at the energy business because, at that time, energy matters were becoming highlighted. Fuel costs were going up and I felt that I had something to offer.'

He went to France and found a product which was fairly unusual at that time: it consisted of a series of plastic strips which hung in a door opening and held heat inside a building. The product was very low-tech, but it was affordable. 'So you could go into a factory, a printing hall or whatever,' Ellickson recalls, 'and offer this strip curtain through which they could drive with a fork-lift truck without getting out of it – just burst through it – and it fell back into place and held in the heat.'

That start-up product led to another – not least because Ellickson believed very strongly in the future of the engineering business and its relevance to where industrial Ireland was headed. 'We were not sophisticated in Ireland in the seventies in engineering terms,' he says, 'so I believed that one fast-track way into technology was to sign a licence. So I signed several licences with American, Canadian and French companies to manufacture their products here. You pay the piper, of course, but you are immediately on to a new level of knowledge, because they are handing you all of their results and the results of their research and development. You could spend a lot of time fooling around on an ego trip and then find out you had run out of money before you had developed a saleable product.

'The route is well catalogued. You see a product you like. You get a distribution agreement for it. You start selling it. It starts to motor. You sign a licence agreement to make it in Ireland, hopefully at a competitive cost, and then you continue on and develop the market. And in some of the cases, North American, Canadian products that they didn't have a market for at home – if you did well, they would say, "Well, why not sell in Europe?"'

The most successful item for Ellickson Engineering was a hydraulic dock leveller. This product is a ramp that rises and puts out a lip on the back of a container and sits down. Then you can drive your fork-lift truck into the container and unload very quickly. Irrespective of the height of the container, this platform will rise and fall and level the factory floor to the container so that the platform is on the factory side. The hydraulic dock leveller can now be seen in almost every cold store, warehouse and factory around the country. Ellickson found it by going to exhibitions, reading magazines and getting information from embassies. 'Every commercial counsellor in every embassy has a vested interest in selling his country's products in the country where he is situated,' he points out.

The dock leveller later became, not a single product, but a brand. It went hand in hand with a seal around the door opening. The container squeezed this foam-filled seal, making an airtight connection between the container and the factory. The slogan was, 'The container became part of the factory'; the new system promised speedier, easier unloading, as opposed to the old method, which, in Dominic Ellickson's description, 'was pallet, truck and two lads talking and chatting and struggling'.

The final piece in the jigsaw was the insulated electric door which closed that opening. When a container arrived, workers were able to press a button, open an electric insulated door, go in to the container and empty that container in ten to twelve minutes. Multiples and cold stores wanted that capacity desperately, because they did not want hot air coming into the building during the summer. All these features became a package around which was developed a branded loading-bay system. This system even featured an electrically operated lock so that, while a fork-lift truck was on the ramp, the container driver could not drive away and thus cause an accident.

Later, when gas was piped ashore in Cork, Ellickson Engineering signed a licence agreement for gas filters with a large company in Toronto and put the same formula to work. As Ellickson notes, 'Nothing turns on an architect or a consultant more than to have a reliable supplier who keeps his promises and delivers what he promised. If they were happy with the product and the client would say, "Yes, the after-sales service is good", then you would get repeat business.'

In the very beginning, Dominic and Noeleen Ellickson were the board of their own company, with Ellickson deciding all policy and operational matters. Later, he appointed two or three internal directors, often because they had been successful as executives within the company. Partly because of their deep involvement with the company, those directors resisted when Ellickson wanted to bring on to the board as a non-executive director a former financial controller of Waterford Crystal. '"He wouldn't know anything about the business", was their objection,' he remembers. 'My point was that this was the very essence of his usefulness. He would have a fresh mind and would question things we took for granted, but no.'

At the time, Ellickson acquiesced, but he never lost his conviction that ignorance of the Ellickson family business on the part of a non-executive director would have been an advantage rather than a disadvantage. Looking back, he now also believes the chairman should not be the managing director as well.

In another company Ellickson helped set up – Tour IT in Dublin – the chairman is Dr Denis Jenning, head of Computer Services at UCD. Ellickson believes the fact that Dr Jenning had not previously worked for the company is a very good thing for the business. 'Dr Jennings is detached,' Ellickson says. 'He doesn't get involved in day-to-day operations and he is a very good chairman. I took on both roles in many of my companies – and regret it. A good CEO should do it their way, but I believe they should be questioned by their chairman as to their motivation in doing things. Indeed, they should be answerable to the board.

'This is wisdom in hindsight, because I never had time to think about it when I was in the swim of things. I think I would have responded well to independent questioning from the chair, because the board meetings we did have were very diplomatic and democratic. Everyone had their say. Everyone had their turn. There was no such thing as Lee Iacocca of Chrysler saying, "Let's hear what you have to say and then I'll make up my mind." No, I felt I had an even-handed way of dealing with issues that made sure people were always on side and felt they were being listened to. I have taken many decisions as a result of my own people's suggestions. I wouldn't for a moment think I would have a problem with a board or a chairman. As time went on, I became chairman of Waterford Airport and joined the board of Tour IT and further companies. It was only then that I saw how a board can work really well.'

One of the characteristics of Dominic Ellickson's business approach has been deliberate fragmentation: creating several small companies rather than one large one. This is a way of keeping each entity vibrant and minimising bureaucracy.

On the other hand, where a family business grows as a single entity so that, after the first decade or so, it has moved from being a small business to a medium-sized business employing anything from twenty to a hundred people – or even a large business – the founder is likely to come under pressure to have a board of directors that fulfils some real functions. It is at this point, in my view, that many business founders miss a golden opportunity. Instead of speculating about what would be the ideal make-up of the ideal board for the company at this time, such a founder, convinced of their own broad-spectrum competence and of the uniqueness of their company, reject the advice of consultants – who always, in my experience, recommend that companies have 'a good, solid board' – and rig up a board made up of those members of their family and friendship circles who are least likely to get in the way of the founder's preferred direction for the company.

In other words, the founder essentially believes he or she can shape the future for the company they established. When this happens, they select board members for one of the following lousy reasons:

- *As a reward.* Several founders have put their parents on their board, not because they propose to listen to them – they don't – but because they have the view that 'My mother/father made me what I am today, and I owe it to them.'

- *As a consolation prize.* This happens when founders are sorry for siblings whose lives they perceive to be dull and unsuccessful.
- *As insurance.* Along the lines of former US president Lyndon Johnson's recommendation that it is better to have a potential enemy inside your tent, pissing out, than outside your tent, pissing in, some founders believe they can remove the sting in a resentful relative's tail by appointing them to the board.
- *As an act of kindness.* Where a relative or old friend has fallen on hard times, a yearly £10,000 director's fee can be seen as charity without the stigma.
- *As kicking upstairs.* The brother – or sister – who is constantly underfoot in the business can sometimes be promoted to the board in the hope that membership thereof will lead to membership of Chambers of Commerce, umbrella bodies of small and medium industries, positions on committees within IBEC or even inclusion in the odd state board or task force: anything, in short, that will get the brother or sister off the plant floor and out of the CEO's hair.

Every one of these reasons can be lethal. Indeed, these reasons, used to justify either the employment or appointment as directors of an individual, have so frequently proved fatal to good family businesses that I believe every family business might usefully have two rules prominently displayed in areas like the board room and the CEO's office:

- *If someone, whether that person be a relative or complete outsider, does not have a specific set of demonstrable competencies which provably match a previously identified set of company needs, we will not give them a job within the company.*
- *If someone, whether that person be a relative or complete outsider, does not have a specific set of demonstrable competencies which provably match a previously identified set of company needs, we will not give them a seat on the company'Board of Directors.*

That kind of statement, if acted upon (as it has been, for example, in the case of the Spanish wine business, Codorníu, see Chapter 10) can deliver enormous benefits: benefits that percolate right down through the company, affecting family and non-family staff alike. However, following such a statement can be hugely problematic when it comes to setting up a board of directors, especially if the family business has been in operation for a couple of generations and a practice has grown up of employing family members based on nothing but DNA. Even if the family business is in the first generation, it isn't easy, partly because of the point made earlier: the CEO, having got this far as a result of personal drive and vision, may not have the imagination to determine which traits or competences will best serve the organisation in the future.

When embarking on a process like this, I would suggest that the first interface worth examining is that between the board and the chief executive. If the board cannot meet the CEO's needs and complement his or her capacities, then, no matter how effective it is on other fronts, the board is unlikely to be successful – at least for the time that that particular CEO is at the top of the business.

The managing director, I believe, should be able to look upon his or her board as a group of advisers, rather than as a group of people to be competed with or circumvented. A good board, for me, is a group of people who can provide guidance to the people who are running the business without rubbing these people's noses in the fact that they are being guided. So the first competence I would seek in board members is that they are reasonably subtle – that they are not showboaters. They should be people who can make suggestions rather than hold forth on what they would do if they held the CEO's post.

The second competence – and, for my money, the single most importance competence all board members should have – is the capacity to motivate. A managing director should look forward to board meetings as stimulating occasions where a wider framework can be fixed around any issue the MD is grappling with, not as oral examinations designed to catch the MD doing something wrong. I know of family-business MDs who wake up on the morning of board meetings with a deep sense of dread.

'I always feel that I'm going to get flak at this meeting because my figures aren't right or whatever,' one managing director says. 'A consultant I had in told me I should just realise that my board members ask me negative questions because they need to show each other that they're on top of the task, but that's no help at all.'

Older board members who have a good deal of business experience behind them should regard themselves as the managing director's mentors and encouragers, not as monthly interrogators. In fact, logically, that is the only role they should fulfil, since they are in effect saying, by coming on to the board when the MD is in position or by appointing the MD, 'This person is the right person for the job.' It mystifies me why some boards seem to work on the belief that the managing director, unless closely monitored and micro-managed, is likely to turn out to be incompetent or corrupt, or both. Many of the men and women running family businesses I interviewed when researching this book confided that, when they run into a negative, suspicious and demotivating board, they cope by concealing things from the board and misdirecting it.

'Not all of my board are bad,' one CEO told me, 'but I have an uncle who has never been in business at all. He's an academic, and he thinks his role is to give me the third degree once a month. None of the rest of them stand up to him, and that brings them down in my estimation, because if you have one board member pursuing some tiny, inconsequential error in the figures down to the last irrelevant decimal point, you're wasting time that should properly be spent on other issues.

'It took me maybe six months to a year to resign myself to the fact that they were all intimidated by him and that they would come to me afterwards and give a mealy-mouthed explanation of why they had let him put me in this mortifying position, even though they personally, of course, knew I was doing a splendid job. What they didn't appreciate was that I was growing to despise them as much as I despised him: him for bullying; them for being crawlers. Eventually, I and my financial controller began to play games with him. He wants a trailing wire to catch hold of and pull on? We'll give him trailing wires!'

This executive now inundates her board with irrelevant data, knowing that the majority of the members will not read it, and seeds the data with one or two 'trailing wires': typos or marginally inaccurate figures. She and her financial controller now wait, at board meetings, with positive if somewhat predatory enjoyment, for the academic to catch and complain about the errors, confident that making deliberate mistakes gives them a bizarre form of control. Of course, she admitted, somewhat shamefacedly, this is a disgraceful waste of time, but what could she do?

Any board member who perceives their function to be to harass the managing director so that he or she is 'kept on their toes' or forced to 'shape up' is grievously mistaken. I would go further. Whenever I have seen this kind of performance, it has transparently been in the interests of the board member's ego, not in the interest of the company. Indeed, it has frequently done damage to the company's interests, as exemplified by my friend who wastes good executive time on her own part and on the part of her financial controller by laying spurious traps for the harassing board member.

The word 'motivate' should be engraved on every board member's heart. They should themselves be motivated to build a great company. They should be committed to motivating the executives who run the company, and to realising that money alone is insufficient to motivate thinking human beings. And I think they should have this ability and commitment, not just as individuals, but as a group. This last point is actually very difficult to achieve: put a bunch of people together around a board table and they often forget that the raw material of business is people – and you can't run people the way you can run engines.

It is also perhaps even more difficult for family members to be effective directors for the reasons already identified:

board members in a family business may have known the managing director since he or she first demonstrated they were tone-deaf or uninterested in sport or since they got drunk at the grandparents' golden wedding. Family members tend to be fairly adept at identifying each other's limitations and deficits. Concentrating on their potential is more difficult.

On the other hand, when it comes to selecting directors for a family business, the reverse may hold true, since, with members of any family that is reasonably close, there is a warts-and-all familiarity. As a result you have a much better idea of what you're getting, if you are the founder, MD or chairman setting out on the selection process, because the chances are you know them, you have been brought up with them, you know what their agendas are and you know what their weaknesses are.

That familiarity notwithstanding, you still need to concentrate on the needs the company has of its board and of the competences each member has, so that, in aggregate, the board will meet those needs. Technically, a board of directors should direct, not manage, the business. Directing the business, as opposed to managing it, means:

- Engaging in strategic planning for the long-term future of the company
- Making policy decisions
- Being involved in the allocation of significant financial resources within the organisation
- Being involved in the allocation of significant financial resources outside the existing organisation, for example, in mergers, acquisitions or external investments

In my own business, for example, there are a number of strategic issues facing all of us who run newspapers. Some of these issues are massive, and largely unquantifiable, such as the long-term impact of the Internet on the industry. Any good board of directors within a family-owned newspaper group will, in the past decade, have looked at a number of strategies for at least coping with, and at best optimising, the growing use of the Internet. It would have been my board of directors which would have made the decision to put the newspaper on the Web every day without charge, but using a registration method in order to track visitors would have come from people running the web site. The implications of the Internet for a newspaper go much further than that, however. One school of thought suggests that people will never abandon the pleasure of opening a broadsheet – or tabloid – chunk of newsprint and visiting their favourite pages.

Let's assume that is what the man in my seat believes. In that case, it is vital that one or more board members pays attention to the convergence of telephones and computers: if, as seems likely, by 2003 the majority of people have access to mobile phones which access the Net easily and cheaply and have high-definition, full-colour screens on which the users can read their favourite newspaper without either the bother of going to a news-stand or the expense of paying for the paper, then that will undoubtedly affect a newspaper's sales.

The capacity to think strategically is a key competence for directors. Strategic thinking is the ability to be curious about possibilities – both negative and positive – in all aspects of the competitive environment surrounding a business. Strategic thinkers tend to look at time in three-

or five-year segments rather than the quarter-by-quarter segments in which day-to-day managers may have to deal. Above all, strategic thinkers are untrammelled by a firm's track record. They never promote a course of action for the company based on the fact that 'this is how we've always done it'. They may be respectful of precedent, but not in awe of it when it comes to planning where the enterprise should go.

Directors must also develop policy for their organisation. This is one of the areas of predictable conflict between boards and executives. The fact that conflict in this area is predictable means that the very word 'policy' should be surrounded by red flashing lights. Put bluntly, at least nine out of ten members of the average board do not know the difference between policy and its implementation. Not only is this failing not confined to family businesses, it is not confined to commercial boards. A recent controversy involving one state board clearly indicated that, whatever the faults the executive of the state agency involved may possess, the more immediate problem is that the members of the board have a deeply flawed understanding of their function: they wish to control the actions of individual staff members and the allocation of quite small sums of money by those staff members in a way which has no bearing on their responsibilities as board members.

A board may decide, for example, that the organisation it directs should have a strong social conscience and be seen as a good corporate citizen. It may even lay down policy as to which kinds of charities should be considered for sponsorship. But it is not appropriate for board members either to barrack the CEO in order to get £500 for their local youth club or to start moaning about the type of lettering used in the charity-gifts section of the annual report.

'I had a knock-down, drag-out row with a board member who used to bawl out very junior staff, either on the phone or in person,' one MD told me. 'Because we're a service industry, she seemed to think that if she came to head office and wasn't recognised by every passing work-placement kid spending three weeks of their transition year with us, this justified her abusing the student and bringing it up at board meetings.'

Another chief executive, this time of a group of diverse coffee shops that are in the process of coming together under one brand, spoke bitterly to me of one of his directors, who, at board meetings, would agree overall policy, then subvert it when it was implemented. 'We agreed a three-year identity-integration action plan,' the CEO explained. 'During those three years, everything from the logo to the layout of the shops to the menus to the kitchen equipment was to change. The directors and shareholders had all started their own cafés, but had seen the potential of a Europe-wide chain that would be instantly identifiable by customers.

'The directors hired a management team with proven expertise in establishing this kind of set-up,' he recalls,'and, during the first year, made all of the major policy decisions which would – and did – lead to a financial bonanza for the owners. However, one of the board could not resist interfering in the implementation of that policy within his own eating houses.'

'He always knew someone who could do that kind of flooring cheaper than the contractor we had hired,' the top executive told me, wearily. 'So every decision ended up being revisited. Similarly, the board had agreed that the coffee shops would be distinguished by a limited but excellent set of distinctive dishes. Six months after this should have been in place, our quality-control inspector would find shops which were under his aegis still offering items from their old menu. He would get shirty, saying we didn't understand the kind of customers he had in such-and-such a town, and I would end up demanding that the chairman berate him at the next board meeting for going back on policy decisions.

'It was costly in terms of time and money and refits, but the worst cost was in terms of staff morale. We had developed this super training programme for the staff who would be serving people, and the next thing we find he's mocking some of the practices we've introduced, because "didn't his people do fine before all this customer-is-king crap was introduced". It was as if he saw the new methods as a criticism of what he had been doing up to then, even though he had been part and parcel of the decision-making that had led to the new methods. It got to such a point that my chairman one day, trying to calm me down over the latest outrage, said, "He's his own worst enemy", and I said, "Not while I'm alive, he isn't!" I wanted him sent on some remedial director course, but I couldn't find one!'

A director who is unclear about the difference between policy and its implementation often finds that basic lack of clarity made worse by outsiders, who sometimes view a director as a kind of manager-cum-ombudsman-cum-general problem-solver. I had not realised this until I became chief executive of Examiner Publications. From that point on, many introductions led immediately to new acquaintances pointing out something the paper was doing wrong, as they saw it. Because I'm combative by nature, half the time I'd have an argument with them just for the hell of it. Sometimes I'd make a note of what they said and, if I remembered, would pass it on without comment to the editor, making it perfectly clear to him that I was not asking for action on this but was simply the postman delivering someone else's letter. The editor would do whatever he thought fit and would never come back to me on it.

On one occasion, a highly placed representative of a foreign government contacted me with a lengthy series of complaints about that morning's paper, which I hadn't got around to reading. As the issue was a sensitive one, I didn't get into an argument but took detailed notes and promised him I would take action on the matter. The quotations he listed were certainly questionable. But, as it turned out, they weren't in the *Examiner*, nor in the *Echo*. He had, as he saw it, gone straight to the top; the only problem was that he had gone straight to the top of the wrong newspaper!

Generally, though, when outsiders go to a director of a company, they not only get a hearing but often a closer one than what they are saying merits. One marketing director of a family-owned business remembered, with a rueful laugh, a distant cousin who had briefly served on his board.

'He was retired,' the marketing director recalls, 'and did nothing but play golf and attend board meetings – in that order. So, at every board meeting, he downloaded what we laughingly called the harvest of wisdom from his most recent golf partners. One day, I remember, he criticised a half-page ad we were running in the trade press, saying it was 'visually busy'. I nearly fell off the chair. This cousin was so colour-blind his wife had to coordinate him every day, so a crit like that would never have passed his lips if it hadn't been uttered by one of his fellow golfers. It turned out one of his regular foursomes had a former creative director of an ad agency on it. Fortunately, we had a great chairman at the time. Just as I was about to erupt, the chairman said, "Let's not have a brisk exchange of prejudices on a non-agenda item", and before we knew it, we were back on track and I had been prevented from saying what I wanted to say, which was, "Visually busy, my arse!"'

When you have board members who think strategically, keep their fingers out of the routine running of the company and both believe the best of the CEO and seek to bring out the best in him or her, then you are blessed. If one or more of the board members is also experienced and expert – the two, unfortunately, are not always synonymous – on investments and finance, then you come close to the ideal. Increasingly, as family businesses face the need to diversify and expand, coupled with the need to stay ahead technologically, they need high-level financial advice. That can be hired. But an individual on the board who can interpret that advice and facilitate the board in their discussions leading to allocation of substantial financial resources to one of a series of competing needs is a great asset.

In some family businesses, the make-up of the board is not decided by competence but is largely based on shareholding. Nonetheless, shareholding per se does not entitle you to a board position. (Minority shareholders have rights, but this is an area where the individual family business should seek legal advice.)

A variation on the traditional board of directors is an executive board or executive committee. This form of governance is used in cases where the company in question is a subsidiary. Where a firm is a subsidiary of a holding company and you have a group of people running that company, if they are members of the board of the subsidiary, that board can be an executive board charged with running the subsidiary. The main board of directors, though, is the holding company board and within the subsidiary is the title of being a director of that company.

As directors of the executive board, members have certain legal and other responsibilities, but the holding-company board also has the same – if not more – responsibilities. At Examiner Publications, we have a management committee which runs the company on a day-to-day basis. Then on top of that we have the board of Examiner Publications and then we have the board of Thomas Crosbie Holdings, the holding company that owns Examiner Publications and a number of other companies.

In fact, the board of Examiner Publications has very little to do because the governance decisions and responsibilities should take place at holding-company level and the day-to-day running and executive decisions take place at the management-committee level. The strategic direction of the *Examiner* is rather complicated because the members of the board of the *Examiner* also form the board of the holding company.

The issue of the public prestige attached to a directorship should not be underestimated. If acquiring this prestige is a person's only motivation for becoming a director, then of course that person should not be appointed to the board.

On the other hand, I think it is important that people are attracted by the prestige associated with being on a board, so a liking for public recognition is not a contra-indication when picking a board of directors.

However a very serious contra-indication is when the position is seen as a reward for service. If you put someone on the board for that reason, you do an injustice to both the individual and the board. You may put the individual in a situation where they are humiliatingly out of their depth but, even more seriously, you devalue the entire board by making an appointment which carries the inevitable implication that the board does not do any real work and that a board position can be a sinecure. That sends wrong messages to everybody in an organisation.

While the orthodox rationale behind boards of directors is as I have outlined it on page 138, I believe that, in some companies, particularly electronics firms, the pyramid of policy becomes somewhat inverted. Policy and direction may come up from the grass roots rather than from the board of directors, simply because, in such companies, full cognisance of the rapidly changing competitive environment is more likely to be found at operational level than at board level. This is even more likely to be the case if perceived wisdom has been followed and prominent business figures from areas other than electronics have been invited to take up positions on the board.

That inverted pyramid also exists within Examiner Publications. Essentially, issues of policy and direction are dealt with by the management team. As a result, quantum leaps in policy, such as the recent change in the name of the paper to *The Irish Examiner* came from the management team, as did the strategy or direction that the company has adopted, the objective of which is to grow the *Examiner* outside the Cork and Munster area.

Because my own board configuration is unorthodox yet highly effective, I am both sceptical of perceived wisdom on this topic and reluctant to lay down the law about what constitutes the ideal board for a family business. It depends very much upon the dynamics between the family members. The ideal dynamic is summed up in the phrase, 'They get on', not, 'They agree on everything', or even, 'They're as alike as two peas in the proverbial pod.' All you need is for people to get on with each other in a reasonably civil way.

After all, whether or not family board members get on with each other determines what kind of person should be appointed to the board from the outside. If they do not get on, there may be a case for putting a psychologist on the board, whereas if they do get on, maybe it should be an expert in finance or marketing.

Another consideration is the times that are in it. Difficult times require a quite different kind of director to easy times, as one family business founder pointed out to me. He and his accountant wife had started their business in the mid-1980s and, at the millennium, were poised for moves into the global marketplace. 'It was then I realised she had been a great financial controller for a recession,' the founder said. 'But she could not adapt to the expansionary thinking needed by a booming economy.'

In another company, one board member decided to finish his term when the company was about to be rationalised. Another board member recalls that, 'He sat down with me and the chairman, recognised what had to be done, didn't like what had to be done but did recognise it and essentially said to me, "I know what you have to do; I understand what you have to do. I am going to back out and let you do it – I don't have the stomach for it." Now to me, as a family shareholder, that was very enlightened thinking and I'll always admire him for that.'

If it is important that board members have distinct and useful competences, it is even more important that the person in the chair have distinct and useful competences. The chairman should have the ability to see all the different points of view on a particular issue and the ability to communicate with all the various types of people around the table.

They should also have a clear and precise understanding of the role of the person in the chair and the skills to conduct a meeting in such a way that it doesn't last forever and leave unfinished business detritus everywhere. A truly wonderful person in the chair is someone who takes the time to understand what makes people tick, because a family business is all about getting people to work together happily. In an ideal situation, a chairperson has the ability to listen to everybody's point of view, the capacity to be open to someone else's anger and the diplomatic sense to pick the good and the bad from it. He or she should also be the natural person people go to with their problems.

Finally, I believe very strongly that there should be a person on the board of a family business whose sole function is to represent the family.

10

―

HOW CODORNÍU GOT
TO THE EIGHTEENTH GENERATION

At this point, it is clear to any reader that there are few
solid rules that apply to each and every family business.
Such businesses differ too much from each other for any
rigid template to apply to all or even most of them. If there
was a single rule which could be applied, the one I would
personally favour is the one in my title: 'Don't leave it to
the children.' Having said that, I have to admit that, in the
course of researching this book, I did find one outstanding
exception to my pet rule: a Barcelona-based winemaking
company called Codorníu.

Codorníu's history as a business goes back to 1551. In
that year, one Jaime Codorníu left a will that mentions
wine presses, barrels and casks. So it is fair to infer that,
at that early time, the family made wine. Just over a century
later, Maria Anna Codorníu, the last of the family line,
married Miguel Raventós and began the process of building
a business empire, using the bride's name. The next great
leap forward for the business came two centuries later
again, when José Raventós developed wanderlust. He
wanted to experience more of the world than was on offer
in his home area, and so he set out for France,
eventually getting as far as the Champagne region in the
far north-east of the country. There, he found wines that

sparkled in a way not found in the wines of his native Penedés.

When he returned home, he began to experiment, and in 1872 he produced a sparkling wine which over the next ten years took the market by storm. His son decided that there was a great international future for the family's sparkling wines and came up with some novel ways to attract public attention to his product. Legend has it that, when it came time to deliver the first vintage of the new wines, he ordered his delivery carts to drive the wrong way up the narrow streets of Barcelona. Chaos ensued, and Codorníu was heavily fined for breaching traffic laws. But Manuel Raventós had achieved his purpose: his product instantly became a talking point.

An early pioneer of advertising, Raventós also organised competitions among the leading artists of Catalonia for posters promoting his wares. He received submissions from painters as eminent as Utrillo. 'Manuel Raventós was more, much more than a pioneer or a clever businessman,' one prestigious wine historian has written. 'He had scientific knowledge and financial structures far superior to those cellar owners who followed his example.'

As this multi-talented man happened along at the right time, by the end of the nineteeth century Codorníu was known all over Spain. In 1904, the King of Spain visited the cellars, and since then the company has been the official supplier of *cava* – the sparkling wines made according to the *méthode traditionnelle* – to the Royal Palace.

Because the Codorníu business is extremely unusual in its total retention, after the eighteenth generation, in the hands of descendants of the first winemaker, I travelled to

Barcelona to meet Maria Raventós, who has been chairman of the company since 1999. Señora Raventós, a tall, slender, comfortably informal blonde, occupies an office that is modest and unpretentious. She works most mornings and tries to spend afternoons with her six children. When she wants to show you something, she goes and gets it herself, rather than calling an assistant.

She explained that she had become chairman as a result of a family council of ten people, two from each branch of the clan, plus the directors of the company. 'They decided this,' she told me, 'because I have worked in the company for twenty-three years. It was important that the person who was chairman knows everything about the company – and the family.'

The person who takes the chair at Codorníu does so for a five-year stretch, after which they can seek to be reappointed if they wish. It could happen, she explained, that a chairperson who wanted to go on for another five years might be told by the family council that they believed it would be better for the company if the chair now went to someone else. The company walks the classic modern tightrope between, on the one side, the imperative of change, and on the other, the need to retain and utilise good people. Maria is clear-headed about the demands of her job, stating that the task is complicated, not least because of the many administrative boards that exist within Codorníu's corporate structure. 'It is not enough to be nice,' she says. 'You have to be multiskilled and independent, know all family members – and be totally committed.'

The managing director, who reports to the chairman, is usually a member of the family, but this is not essential, as in the case of the chairman. Ambitious professional managers who join the company therefore do not have their expectations stunted by the belief that they can never make it to the top. The present managing director is a member of the family but at some future time the position could be filled by a non-family professional.

In recent years, the company has also taken a person from outside the family onto the board of directors – a move which at the time caused many of the family to look doubtfully at the director involved. 'That was seen as quite dangerous – quite risky: to put one non-family member on the board. It began in 1993, and for the moment he is a very good director, so we are very pleased with him. He is the only one that is not in the family.'

Listening to the Codorníu family saga, one is constantly impressed by the fact that, while there are rules, there is little rigidity about the application of those rules. Rather, there is a constant awareness of how much everything in the business world is changing.

Nothing is hard and fast at Codorníu. If something is in the interest of the company, they will do it. Sometimes, when I asked about rules, Maria looked at me questioningly – so surprised by the word that I wondered whether her reaction was due to the fact that she is Spanish or was characteristic only of her particular company. Clearly, if the Raventós family want to break their own rules, they're going to break the rules. However, this flexibility in attitude must be seen against the conscious attitude of rectitude that is demanded of family members who serve on the board or on the staff. Of them the highest expectations are held.

The Codorníu philosophy seems to be that it is a good thing to have a few big rules rather than a plethora of small rules, strictly applied, which could not, by their very nature, take account of the people and the moment within which those people work. On the other hand, the company chairman constantly reiterates the need for communication at all levels. 'Tell the family what you're doing' is a guideline to which Señora Raventós adheres with an infectious fervour.

Rigidity and the desire to control from the grave are rarely to be seen in Codorníu. Professionalism and communication, on the other hand, are highly valued and prioritised. 'I think it's important,' says Maria, 'to be very professional in the company, to communicate and, above all, to be very honest. That is very important for the shareholders and for the people who work in the company and for the clients. Our behaviour has to match the quality of our product. That is an idea that is very important to me.'

Codorníu now has 144 shareholders, all family members, although only seven family members work in the company. The scarcity of family members is due to a company protocol which lays down rules for how family members can become executives. Having very good English is the first requirement: this is seen as very important because English is effectively the language of business. The next requirement is a university degree: 'a very high degree', Maria explains.

Then, the person must have worked for five years in a company other than Codorníu – and have been a success in that other company. When I ask Maria who defines whether or not a person has been a success, Maria lets out a long, slow 'Aaah' and smiles. This undoubtedly is – or has been – an issue for the company. The answer is that a family council – which is made up of two members of the family who work within the family firm, two other members who work elsewhere, and two people with MBAs or similar qualifications who are perceived as having expertise – is called in on the selection of family members for the family business.

This arrangement sounds more complicated than, in practice, it is. The bottom line is that, as a family member, you know the requirements almost from the day you're born. There is no 'silver spoon' sense of entitlement to a job. As a family member, you are entitled to a shareholding – but not a job.

If, having achieved good English, got an appropriate degree under your belt and worked successfully in another company, you then decide you want to work in Codorníu, you telephone the family council and tell them so. They then interview you and make a recommendation for or against you, on the basis of the interview. The process is demanding, thorough and oddly detached. Even though everything is carried out within the family, it is kept free of emotion, and the priority is always the short- and long-term needs of the company rather than the preferences of the individual.

'What is most important for the company is that it makes a good profit,' Maria Raventós says. 'That is most important for the shareholders. Everybody from the family cannot work in the company. That would be impossible, because we have so many people in the family. Anyway, the company has to be directed by professional people. They may be shareholders or not shareholders, but they *must* be professionals.'

What each branch of the family does with its shareholding pretty much amounts to the preferences of the shareholder in each generation. There is no obligation on them to divide their shares evenly among their children, although Maria, who has six children, has passed on equal shareholdings to each of them, believing this to be 'the most just thing for the family'. She also believes that the shareholdings should be passed on to the children as early as possible, rather than there being a wait for each generation to die. (In this country, of course, that would attract Capital Acquisitions Tax, but more about that later.)

I questioned this, wondering aloud, when talking with her, whether this approach was necessarily 'the most just thing' for the business. She seemed surprised by the possibility that it might *not* be good for the business, protesting that each individual in the family had the possibility to be a good shareholder. The implication was that members of the Raventós family are brought up almost from birth with an awareness of what it is to be a good shareholder – and take pleasure in fulfilling this role.

'I think that they like the company,' she says simply. Then, after a pause, she adds that, 'If you have a son who is very problematic . . . well, you have to think about that. Normally we don't have these kind of problems I think it is important to give each one the same thing. I think it is better to give responsibility and freedom to the children and then give all the shareholdings to them.'

All shareholdings pay dividends, and any shareholder who wants to can attend the statutory AGM, although in practice, the turnout rarely exceeds twenty. In addition to that shareholders' meeting, there is, in September each year, a family meeting which sets out to be more geared to providing information, with some executives explaining aspects of company operations ranging from how investments are made to the rules about how to go about getting a job with the company. At the September meeting all the TV advertisements planned for the upcoming season are shown for the first time, since it is felt to be important that the first non-executive people to see the TV commercials are always members of the family. Anyone within the family who is older than eighteen can attend these meetings, even if they're not shareholders.

'This meeting runs from 11 o'clock until half past one, after which we have a visit to one of the wineries. There is a tour and then we have a meal and a small gift for everybody by which they will remember this day. And that family meeting is very important for us, because you know you can speak with all the people and transmit all the ideas that you have. You can emphasise that quality is the most important factor and let everybody see how well we work.'

Maria Raventós does not underestimate the problems which have emerged, now and again, when a family member has proved unequal to the tasks presented to them as an executive within the company. But all of these problems are solvable, she maintains. She notes that you simply have to explain to the individual or relatives that the action had to be taken because, for the whole family, the most important objective is that the company make a good profit.

Due to sustained profits, shareholders are not as eager to cash in their shares as they might be if they owned part of a publicly floated company. In order to take account of those who wish to sell, however, at the meeting in September the family decide the share price, so that anyone who wishes to dispose of what they own can do so at a transparent price to other family members.

What is particularly elegant about the Codorníu model is that transparency is not seen as sufficient. The balance within the company is kept scrupulously even. If, at any point, one branch of the family is seen as losing out, they get preference to buy shares coming up for sale. If that branch of the family does not buy the shares and it is felt that their purchase by another branch would exacerbate the perceived imbalance, Codorníu has a holding company that buys the shares. As a result, the equilibrium is always maintained. No section of the family can become too powerful, in terms of its shareholding.

The dividend on the shareholding is rather higher than would be standard in a public company. The end result is that a shareholder who is neither on the board of directors nor a member of staff still gains substantially every year from the profits generated by the company and is kept informed of all developments.

Selling shares outside the family is not permitted, and no shareholder is allowed to own more than 10 per cent of the company. Both rules help maintain the company as a family-owned and family-operated business. At the beginning of the twenty-first century, the most significant shareholding in the hands of any individual was 3.2 per cent, with many of the family owning a share as small as 0.8 per cent.

What is fascinating about the Codorníu *cava* business is that, while they seem to have a constantly positive expectation of each other as family members, the shareholders have also evolved an incredibly elaborate system of checks and balances. This system is designed not simply to prevent any one member of the clan from losing the run of themselves and trying to take over or misdirect the enterprise but also to prevent any *branch* of the family from doing anything along those lines.

For example, within each family branch there are two council members, who may or may not have worked in the company. This council has nothing to do with the running of the company; it is more involved in what might be called the running of the family. If any two members of the family raise an issue with which the rest of the council is not in immediate agreement, the matter is put in abeyance. If this issue resurfaces, say, two years later, the council may opt to look into it again before deciding for or against it.

Thus far, there have been few problems with this system, although in 1983 one branch of the family decided they did not like the way in which the company was being run, and sold all their shares to the holding company. That branch set up a winery across the road. This posed no problems to Maria Raventós. As far as she's concerned, that's business. Outsiders who later spotted her dining companionably with the dissident branch were mystified as to why she would continue to be on good terms with them after they had left the family business. 'I say, one issue is professional, and the other thing is my family,' she asserts. 'I could not stop being friends with them, when I have been friends with them all my life – when I played with them as children. I think it's a nice thing – to be able to make the distinction between what is the job or what is the company and what is the family. They are quite different things.'

Although Maria is comfortable with her capacity to separate family relationships from business issues, she laughingly admits that a newcomer marrying into the family may feel that, rather than marrying one husband or wife, they are marrying 144. That sense of marrying into a family which is also a huge business must be reinforced by pleasant company rituals. For example, if a member of the family has a baby, she receives a case with twenty-four bottles of *cava* with a label dedicating it to the new baby. New products, too, are given to family members first because it is felt that they should be the first people to know and taste company wares. Endless thought goes into making the shareholders feel special, even if their individual shareholding is small.

High standards of personal and private behaviour are demanded of board members, but the same standards are not applied to shareholders. It is as if board members must consider themselves, like Caesar's wife, to be above reproach, whereas shareholders are commoners, and thus free to behave as they wish. So if a shareholder runs into a financial problem and that difficulty causes them to want to sell the shares, there is a market for that equity within the family.

'We are quite a normal family,' Maria Raventós stresses, improbably. 'We don't like to have problems – the only thing that we like is to work and to work well.' Differences in personality are absorbed, whether on the part of the president (chairman) or managing director. Indeed, Maria believes that the five-yearly changes arising from new people taking up top posts are good for the company.

On the other hand, she is completely against the problems of family members being allowed to get to the people who are in the business of running the company on a day-to-day basis. So she created – and for a while headed

– a department specifically designed to resolve problems associated with shareholders without taking up the time of the people who are mandated to create profits for the shareholders. This is an interesting concept, which, one feels, might have made a profound and positive contribution to the troubled histories of once-proud family businesses nearer home.

As I mentioned earlier, the fact that top management concentrate on generating profit means that, although the dividend varies from year to year in size and in structure, shareholders are for the most part kept happy. Nonetheless, I did point out to Señora Raventós that, while this profit share-out is possible in this, the eighteenth generation, in the nineteenth or twentieth generation, given the constant dividing up of shareholdings among the offspring of the present owners, Codorníu could fairly soon get to a stage where every shareholder has 0.0001 per cent of the business, with commensurately small dividends accruing. She is well aware that when individual shareholders have grown up with the expectation of substantial dividends, then, should the dividend ever shrink markedly, all bets would be off and the agenda would radically change.

'It is for that reason we concentrate on expanding the company,' she said, nodding. 'It is for that reason we bought in a winery in Argentina, we bought in the Napa Valley in California and in other locations, including Rioja. It is all to make more profit and to make the company bigger. It is a real problem. You have to think about how much money [you want to use] for investment, while at the same time ensuring a high enough dividend for the shareholders. If you do not designate and lay aside enough money for investment, in the short term you may have a lot of money for the shareholders, but in the medium to long term, you are going to run into a problem because the numbers of shareholders and their demands is going to outstrip what the company can generate.'

Or, to put it more crudely, the weight of shareholder expectation – the hunger of multiple-shareholder need – could, if all did not go well, bring down the company. That prospect is not seen by the firm's chairman as an immediate threat but rather as a pressure which may become heavier in the next generation. In her view, even that pressure does not outweigh the benefits and joys of being part of a family business, however. 'You just have to remember,' she says, 'that you have a responsibility to the next generation.' In a variation on the Crosbie-family mantra that the business is borrowed by each generation for handing on, in improved condition, to the next, the members of the Raventós family try, in each generation, to be better than their parents in the way they operate the business.

That determination to match or do better than previous generations undoubtedly played a part in the way the family broke with Spanish tradition in having a female president – Maria's grandmother – several decades ago. This is not to say, however, that the old sexist ways don't surface now and again.

'I think it is a good thing to be a woman in this company,' Maria notes. 'Here we have very good opportunities. But inevitably, if one day you say you have to stay at home because you have a child that is ill, people say "Ah, that's women." Of course, if a man says, "I am going to play golf", nothing happens – nobody makes a judgement. That is normal in Spain and in many countries. So you have to work hard. I am very proud of all the women that work in this company – not because I am a woman but because the women work very hard and very well.'

Maria Raventós believes that having family members in the company who are seen to 'work very hard and very well' has major implications for staff attitudes. Mentioning the long hours she herself works, she indicates that this allows her to ask for strong performance from her staff. If it is useful to have family members within the company, it is also perceived within the family – and registered within their protocols – that the numbers of these people should be kept low, however. Normally, they say that 1 per cent of all the people who work in all the group should be family members. At present, Codorníu's workforce numbers in toto about 800 people, of whom seven are family members.

Codorníu is an object lesson in the successful management of tradition and change. Its protocols are infinitely subtle in the way they guarantee equilibrium and guard against the worst excesses of family warfare. But what makes the company's efforts such an agreeable exception to much that is bad in family businesses is that, underpinning all of its practices and decisions, is an assumption that relationships within the family are precious and worth sustaining, that disagreements can be absorbed and solved within a healthy family and that quality, pride and profit can happily go together.

In one sense, Codorníu is a prime exemplar of the family constitution in action. Philip Smyth, a partner specialising in family business within BDO Simpson Xavier, maintains that 'the cost and anguish of sibling rivalry and well-publicised rifts in high-profile Irish family businesses could have been avoided if the founders had prepared a formal family constitution, setting out a family's strategy for dealing with all the issues that will arise in the life cycle of the business.'

Smyth believes that these are the benefits of having a family business constitution:

- It facilitates the development and documentation of the family's strategic plans for their involvement in the business.
- It is a powerful tool in motivating family and non-family members to strive to play their part in ensuring success.
- It creates the right atmosphere in which to allow the next generation to decide whether to enter the family business and how they should prepare for the roles they will be expected to play in it.
- It allows the family to tap into all the talent available to it. When people know what roles they can realistically aspire to, it helps them to focus more constructively on what they should be doing.
- It provides for governance of the business in areas such as the role and function of the board of directors and who should be directors, and the role, if any, of non-executive directors.
- It specifies remuneration levels for directors, management and family and non-family employees.
- It provides the critical foundation to enable a family business to prepare a robust and achievable business plan that is consistent with the combined objectives of the wider family.

11

Fairy Tales of Letting Go

Now, children, are we sitting comfortably? Then I'll begin. Once upon a time, there was a landowner who owned a huge estate. On the estate there was one house which had no farm attached. In that little house lived the Buggins family.

Now, the Buggins family were tenants. That meant they had to pay rent to the great landowner. But the Buggins family were not farmers. They just lived in the little house. They had an income, though.

The income came from their golden apple. Many years before, their grandfather had created the most beautiful golden apple, and people came from all over the country to see it. The visitors paid the Buggins a fee in order to get to see their golden apple. The Buggins kept the fees in a jar, and at the end of the year they paid the landlord's rent out of that jar.

The landlord and the Buggins family lived very happily in this way for many, many years. Then one day, just after the business had passed to a new generation, the new landlord visited the Buggins family home.

'I want to take a bite out of your golden apple,' he told the family.

'But if anybody ever takes a bite out of our golden apple, the rest of the apple will tarnish immediately,' the Buggins family said. 'Our grandfather told us we must never let anyone bite it.'

'I just want to take a bite out of your golden apple,' the landlord said. 'I don't want to hear arguments about it.'

So the landlord took a bite of the apple and went away. Not long afterwards, the apple began to tarnish, and within a month it was a stained, ugly remnant of what it had been. Visitors who came to look at it refused to pay. When the visitors went away from the Buggins house, they warned other visitors, and so, as the weeks went on, the flow of visitors dwindled to a trickle and then stopped completely.

The generation of the Buggins family who had so recently inherited the golden apple now had no income to put in their jar and, at the end of the year, no money to pay the landlord.

'You made us lose our income,' they explained when he demanded money from them. 'You insisted on taking a bite of our golden apple and that caused it to tarnish, so now it's ugly.'

'I wanted the bite,' the landlord said.

'And it didn't matter to you that you took away our livelihood,' the Buggins family said sadly.

'I'll evict you,' the landlord said. 'Sooner or later, someone else will come along, and I'll rent your house to them.'

But nobody ever did rent the house because there was no means to pay the rent and the house became a ruin. No child would want to hear such a sad, pointless story.

This tale is, however, a sad, pointless story that gets played out somewhere in this country every week, between the state (the landlord) and family businesses (the Buggins). Central to it is an iniquitous tax called Capital Acquisitions

Tax. This tax means that any entrepreneur who creates Golden Apple Ltd, builds it into a sizeable and profitable business and then wants to give that business to his or her children could, in the process, destroy the golden apple.

Most family-business owners are not cash-rich. They don't have lots of 'back-pocket money'. They have the asset of the family business, but they may not even pay themselves high wages. Accordingly, unless they have money from some other source, Capital Acquisitions Tax can mean that they have to sell off – or financially weaken – the business in order to make the money to pay the tax that is due when they receive the company from their parent.

Capital Acquisitions Tax is often regarded by people who have never inherited a business as something rich people complain about, when they can well afford to pay it. Rich people don't ever take a positive attitude to paying taxes. Indeed, Sir James Goldsmith, who left to his eight heirs not a family business but a cash fortune, reputed to have been worth in the region of £1.5 billion, flew out of France when he was on his deathbed rather than pay that country's inheritance tax.

The problem with Capital Acquisitions Tax is not about preferences but about whether it is a legitimate tax at all. It is a matter of right or wrong. In my view, not only is not right – it's an outrage. To paraphrase another businessman, it's anti-enterprise, it's anti-family, it's anti-employee, it's anti-logic, it's anti-bloody everything.

It's particularly anti-employee, and I believe trade unions should campaign against it because it threatens employment.

Even if the inheriting generation does not have to sell off the business in its entirety in order to find the money to pay the tax, they will usually have to borrow against the firm, which means finding savings within the business in order to service the debt. This in turn means either that staff numbers are cut or that staff salaries are constrained.

There are, of course, a few specific reliefs available to individuals on the transfer of a family business to a child. One of those reliefs is related to retirement. In order to qualify for retirement relief, the parent has to be over fifty-five when the shareholdings pass hands, and the parent must have owned the assets or shares in the family company for a minimum of ten years. A drawback, as far as I'm concerned, to this particular relief, is that the parent does not actually have to retire. The parent could hand over most, if not all, of the business to a child or children, but still be effectively running the business. Bearing in mind that I have argued, repeatedly, in this book that there are no hard-and-fast rules applying to all family businesses, I am wary of saying that a parent hanging on to control of a company is always going to be a bad thing. Nonetheless, it does run counter to one of my personal rules: *people who have run family businesses should let go of them completely when they let go.*

Moving upstairs in the hierarchy, to a more prestigious title, but staying, like a skeleton at the feast, while your children try to steer the business in a new direction to meet new needs rarely works. Having said that, of course, there are numerous exceptions to this rule. A good example of such an exception is the Morgan car-making company.

But then, Morgan is an exception to almost every rule. At a time when European car manufacturers cannot break even unless they sell millions of vehicles every year, Morgan makes profits of £3 million by selling 600 cars a year. Almost a century after Ford invented the assembly line, Morgan regard themselves as having modernised by changing from starting ten cars on a Monday to starting two cars each day of the week. (On Mondays, they acknowledge, things used to get a bit crowded and there wasn't much space to work.) At a time when automated mass production is standard throughout the automotive industry, Morgan still carry out most of the manufacturing stages in the production of their cars by hand.

The Morgan company, which has been based in the Malvern Hills since the beginning of the last century, was the brainchild of H. F. S. Morgan, the founder and inventor of something called sliding-pillar front suspension, which gave Morgan cars good road grip but did tend to rattle the driver's fillings. The company built an international reputation – 50 per cent of its output is exported – for its beautifully crafted, leather-upholstered, low-slung cars. Morgan aficionados are, to this day, prepared not only to pay £60,000 for the latest model but to wait up to four years for the handcrafted car to be delivered.

Ten years ago, Sir John Harvey-Jones's TV business programme, *Troubleshooters*, came to the Morgan plant and made what have been described as 'blistering criticisms' of its operations. The Morgan company has made changes in the interim, although, as Harvey-Jones found when he recently revisited the company's factory, most of these changes are decidedly *not* the ones he recommended. Indeed, most of them are relatively minor; like, for example, lunchtime cover. Traditionally, if you telephoned Morgan at lunchtime, you got no answer, because all of the workforce lived near the plant and went home for lunch.

Now, someone mans the phone through lunch. In addition, the company has cut, from four weeks to less than three, the length of time it takes to make a car. This is not revolutionary, but such measured, incremental change is part of the character of Morgan as an enterprise, as well as being part of the unique sales appeal of the brand, to those in the know.

Today, the company is run by Charles Morgan, who is as protective about the company's reputation and as defensive in the face of criticisms as if he had started to work there the moment he left school. But what is different about Charles Morgan is that he did not go into the car-making business after school. In a pattern currently being replicated throughout family businesses worldwide, he initially carved out a career that was light years away from car-making. He became an ITN cameraman, having done a degree in business management. His father, Peter, has gone against my rule of 100 per cent handover. He is still around the business but is 'taking it easier' now that he is in his eighties.

Charles Morgan is the personification of a major trend, confirmed in 2000 by the first comprehensive survey of the dynamics and attitudes of family businesses. The survey, commissioned by accountants Grant Thornton and undertaken by Sue Birley, professor of entrepreneurship at Imperial College in London, looked at family businesses in sixteen countries. It found that children of family entrepreneurs are much more likely these days than in the past to pursue career opportunities outside the family business. 'There will always be people who want family to be involved in the business,' Professor Birley admits, 'but what is changing is the expectations both of the family and the children.'

Roughly a quarter of the British entrepreneurs polled said they did not expect their children to go into the family business. This does not quite match up with the findings of another survey, which found that twice that number of entrepreneurs' children did not plan to go into the family firm. That said, at the moment, 78 per cent of owner-managers of family businesses have worked in other businesses; but, of course, they did eventually head for home.

Birley noted this, saying that, while some offspring initially wanted to go off, get a degree and work in any business other than the one started by their parents or grandparents, many of them were eventually attracted back into it. She regards this as a very positive trend. 'You are seeing a different sort of family business emerging. People are working elsewhere before joining the family firm; [they are] joining later and getting MBAs.'

She's right. The next generation is spreading its wings, finding out what it's like to work in quite different businesses, learning that the methods, assumptions and corporate culture that characterise their family business do not necessarily represent best practice. If they return to the business, they may be capable of much more detached and strategic thinking than if they had gone into it as their first job. In addition, they will almost certainly be able to negotiate with other family members in the business from a position of externally gained strength and insight.

It is debatable, however, that this will endear them to the founders or owner-managers, or make the transition into retirement or semi-retirement easier for those owner-managers. Notwithstanding the comments I made earlier about Capital Acquisitions Tax, the fact is that most of the problems owner-managers have in letting go of their business, either to outsiders or to the next generation in the family, arise from the question of loss of control rather than loss of wealth. To be central to an enterprise – to be the person making all the major decisions – can be addictive, despite all the complaints owner-managers make about having to work all the hours God sends and having nobody to whom to delegate.

In an ideal world, owner-managers should, as they face the succession issue, start to improve their personal skills, because this transition to a new role requires skills they may never have needed up to now, like the skill of *not* making a decision or of *not* giving advice. One younger manager told me that his father's problems in managing the transition were painful to watch. 'My dad is not one of those people who can't bear to let go,' the younger manager says. 'He had no problem letting go. He did it in an almost picture-perfect way. Except for one thing. Whenever a problem surfaced that my sister and I, as joint managing directors, brought to his attention, he went into an agony over his inability to come up with an instant and perfect solution. He's not good at being a sounding board, because his first reaction is, "I can't solve that for you", when what you want is not a solution but just a listening ear – a place where you can talk out a problem, knowing that you are likely, as you hear yourself talk, to come up with the solution yourself. I want him to be there, but I want him there to facilitate me finding my own solutions.'

Owner-managers, approaching the point where they will hand over their business, may need training to develop a different set of listening skills. They may need to learn how to brainstorm with a group rather than to direct group thinking. They may need training in how to ask the simple – even stupid – questions and in how to damp down the reflex of always producing the answers. They may need training in facilitating their successors in reaching their own solutions to problems rather than either coming up with their own solutions or worrying about failing to come up with them.

Succession and transition to retirement present a radically different challenge to able men and women: a challenge that has rarely been identified as an important career phase that demands preparation and up-skilling. In fact, letting go of control – never mind shareholding – in a family business is so problematic that it has provided the poisonous core to fairy tales for generations.

You may not have noticed, but if you think about it, many of the stories we tell our children are about family businesses – and particularly about the challenge of letting go. Take 'Snow White'. *Two* family businesses are involved in that story. There's the seven dwarfs hey ho-ing off to work in the family gold mine every day. They have no clear management structure, but a lot of diversity – the mix of Happy, Sleepy, Sneezy and so on makes up almost the perfect board of directors, although I have reservations about Grumpy's mutterings about 'Wimmen!'

The Seven Dwarf Mining Company lacks good management structure, manufacturing systems and safety standards. They are likely to get into trouble with the Health and Safety Authority, because they have muck and detritus everywhere – until Snow White comes along, because of a catastrophe in her own family business.

A stepmother has taken over. If this woman's talents as a stepmother are minimal, her qualifications to run the business are even fewer. There have to be question marks over any CEO who spends so much time talking to a mirror and developing paranoid notions as a result of what she thinks the mirror is saying to her.

I think there's a really good reason for the fact that so many fairy tales are based around family businesses. The reason is the drama, conflict, bloody-mindedness, excitement, tragedy and financial disaster involved, for founders or owner-managers, in letting go of their business.

There are, for example, business founders who decide to divide the cake evenly down to the last, squashy crumb and who take advantage of all the tax reliefs in order not to cripple the business through Capital Acquisitions Tax but, having divvied out the cake, *will not go away*. They cannot fully let go. They believe they can have it both ways.

This incapacity to let go is exacerbated when the company is moving outside of family hands, because, like religious orders whose diminishing numbers require them to cede large components of their operations to laypeople, they still hope to perpetuate the ethos and uniqueness of the business as it was in their time. Very often, this harking back to mom-and-pop days is a major irritation for the new owners and operators. But not always – as the Sara Lee story shows.

Like many family-business founders, Charles Lubin, a Chicago baker, named a product after his daughter. Then he went a step further and named his business, founded in 1935, after her: Kitchens of Sara Lee.

Lubin *père* was a good enough baker to attract the custom of a man in Texas who wanted some of Sara Lee's baked goods sent to his home. Baked goods do not travel well, but Lubin, spotting the opportunity, changed some of the ingredients so that the end products could be frozen, and by the early 1950s he had a flourishing frozen-food business going. Making the move from a local to a national business was facilitated by Lubin's emphasis on ultramodern plant, research and development and drafting in the creator of the musical *Man of La Mancha* to write the company's advertising jingle. In 1956, he was bought out by Consolidated Foods Corporation, and that, in theory, might have been the end of Lubin and Sara Lee as a name. Except that Consolidated Foods, thirty years after they had taken over Lubin's business, decided that they wanted to have a consumer-friendly title for their overall operation and opted for Sara Lee Corporation.

As Sara Lee, the business went global, opening factories in Australia and Canada and setting up in Britain in the 1970s. Although the family business had been in food, the company name eventually covered a conglomerate of businesses ranging from Kiwi shoe polish to Pretty Polly tights and Brylcreem hair products.

Sara Lee is an example of a corporation in which the founder knew when to let go – but the business knew when to continue to appear to be a family business. In addition to using the name of the founder's daughter as the name of the whole corporation, they went a step further, using the founder's daughter, until very recently, in TV commercials that underlined the family-business roots of the now-global giant.

Unfortunately, not all family businesses have a name as cheerfully domestic as Sara Lee, a founder who can let go as straightforwardly as Lubin seems to have done, or an outsider with the respect for name and ethos shown by the corporation which took over Kitchens of Sara Lee.

Circumstances change cases: particularly circumstances that could not have been anticipated. One Irish family business owner who talked to me during the writing of this book had planned that his eldest son would take over the business. The eldest boy had a real interest in the business and possessed all the talents that would have fitted him for the succession. While still in his teens, however, he died in a road accident. Since none of the remaining brothers and sisters wanted to take over the business, the founder facilitated a management buyout, on the assumption that he would gradually ease his way out of his own business – an assumption fostered by his reaching a legal agreement that he would be paid an annual consultancy fee for a number of years after the company changed hands.

To his astonishment, as soon as the deal was signed, he received a communication from the new managing director indicating that, while the company would of course pay the consultancy fee, they would not actually require him to do anything for them in the coming years. 'It was a bit traumatic,' the founder now admits. 'I had got a good price, and there was no trauma in not being in contact with the MD. But I did regret being separated from the good workers who were there, because they were super guys. They still come back to me for advice if they are having problems – personal or business – and I'm always available to them. But I keep out of the plant. I have not been there since I left!'

What might have been a gradual and easy transition was, in this instance, experienced by the founder as a brutal parting. The new managing director may have felt he could not cope with the ongoing presence of the man who had created and made a huge success out of the business, particularly since the founder was a charismatic and forceful personality. It seems a pity, though, that in order to have a complete sense of being in control, he had to gut the business of one of its strongest assets.

Sometimes, outsiders coming into a business do precisely that: gut the very asset they should most respect. Let me give you an example: Company A, set up by Mr A and inherited by Ms B, Mr C, Ms D and Mr E.

Bright people, all of them. They work out that they need external help. They hire a top-level manager to get Company A into shape for the future. The top-level manager is ruthlessly good at his job. As he is ruthlessly good at his job, he establishes and states that, in the interest of the business, some from among Ms B, Mr C, Ms D and Mr E should not be executives. Seeing his point, they go elsewhere and develop other interests.

So, do they all live happily ever after? No, they don't. When you denude a company of family – strip them out of it completely – it may make the company more efficient, but it also changes the nature of the company entirely.

Family businesses can take the long view. They can sacrifice profit levels *now* in the interest of other, long-term objectives. The company does not have to report to shareholders who want profits right now – and there is a new generation of share-punters in Ireland since Eircom was floated. People who never envisaged calling themselves 'shareholders' in anything other than a pension scheme or their own business are now buying shares. Most of the new shareholders want one of two end results from their purchase. First, they want the share to increase in value so that they might sell it at a profit, or the share-purchaser wants the share to deliver profits so that a dividend can be paid every six months.

An uninvolved shareholder wants profits, and that can shorten the time frame in which they operate. Nobody buys shares in a company in order to get profits two or three years later, and a shareholder who wanted to see profit and be paid a dividend within months of the purchase will not look kindly on profit warnings or explanations that, because so much investment is needed in plant or research or restructuring, profits cannot be expected for months or years. A family shareholder, in sharp contrast, is likely to take the longer view and have the patience necessary to wait out any lean years that occur.

An outsider coming into a family business – as, say, financial controller or general manager – should never misunderstand what is being ceded to them. The family are giving up some control, but it is still a family business. There are no external shareholders to be satisfied every quarter. The business is not going to be monitored by dozens of fund managers whose own reputation, not to mention compensation, depends on the performance of the company. It is an unwise and short-sighted external general manager who will completely eliminate family members from a role in which they can contribute o the business. The immediate gratification of getti g rid of interfering or potentially interfering kin may not last. If you remove all the family members from active involvement in the business, the company may still be a family business in name, but it is no longer a family business in terms of its philosophy.

If you are a family member who is no longer involved in shaping the business, your interest narrows. It comes down to money. Either you focus on the dividend, and you want it to be bigger and surer each year, or, more likely, your priority shifts completely to, 'Let's get the company ready to sell.' This requires a new concentration on profit-making in order to make it an attractive purchase. So, even while the company is still a family business in name, once it gets into this cycle of preparation for possible sale, it is really not a family business any more – and, as a result of forcing family members to let go, the outside manager who started the divesting process may suffer.

That is what happened with the Guy Gannett Corporation, a big media conglomerate on the East Coast of the US. Guy Gannett brought in a man named Jim Schafer, who allowed all family members to end their active involvement in the business, in the process making the company more efficient. The bad news was that this action changed the agendas of the family members. Now they were not drawing salaries or getting a daily kick out of involvement in running the thing, they figured they could do better by selling it off. They duly instructed Jim Schafer to prepare the firm to be sold off, which he did. The company was sold, and thus ceased to be a family business. In the process, however, it ceased to be an employer of Jim Schafer, who ended up out of a job. Jim was quickly snapped up because he is a superb manager. But he would ruefully reflect that family business does need some family members in executive positions.

This is a pattern any outside manager brought in to a family business should not lose sight of. While it may be a very good thing to get rid of family members who are there because of their name rather than because of their ability, it may be unwise to try to get rid of the whole family, because that changes the nature of the business completely, even if the family members still own it. If you are an outsider who has joined the management of such a company, you may be well advised to try to keep the company in family ownership rather than persuading all members of the clan to let go.

Postscript

At the beginning of *Anna Karenina*, Tolstoy wrote that while happy families resemble each other, every unhappy family is unique in its misery. The same point can be made about family businesses. The ones which are successful down through the generations tend to have much in common. The ones which fail are often unique in the ways in which they acrimoniously self-destruct.

In researching this book, only one personal certainty of mine has been reinforced. I was pretty sure, when I started out, that virtually no single rule that could be applied in one family business would have the same effect in another such business. By their very nature, family business are not amenable to generalisations.

If you are part of a family business, you may already have experienced the way in which such firms produce in you the full range of emotions, from delirious happiness to abject misery. If you want to sustain your family business in fun and profit – the only two justifications for any business – then keep in mind a variation on the old advice given to people going into property, who are told, 'There are three things that matter in real estate: location, location, location.'

When it comes to family businesses, there are three things that count: communication, communication, communication.

BIBLIOGRAPHY

Baldwin, Neil. *Edison – Inventing the Century*. New York: Hyperion, 1995.

Collier, Peter and David Horowitz. *The Kennedys: An American Drama*. New York: Summit Books, a division of Simon and Schuster, 1985.

Forbes, Malcolm. *What Happened to Their Kids?* Simon and Schuster: New York, 1990.

Hamer, Dean and Peter Copeland. *Living with Our Genes*. New York: Doubleday, 1998.

Harris, Judith Rich. *The Nurture Assumption*. Free Press: New York, 1998.

Lacey, Robert. *Ford: The Men and the Machine*. Little, Brown: Boston and Toronto, 1986.

Levine, Joshua. *The Rise and Fall of the House of Barneys*. New York: William Morrow, 1999.

Packard, David. *The HP Way: How Bill Hewlett and I Built Our Company*. New York: HarperBusiness, 1995.

Tifft, Susan E. and Alex S. Jones. *The Patriarch: The Rise and Fall of the Bingham Dynasty*. New York: Summit Books, a division of Simon and Schuster, 1990.

INDEX

Fleet Street, 10
Ford, Edsel, 32
Ford, Henry, 13-5, 24
    as father, 32

Gannett, Guy, 181
Gates, Bill, 90, 128
Gettysburg Address, the, 10, 26
Goldstein, David, 101-2
Graham, Phil, 35
Graham, Katharine, 34-5
Grant Thornton Accountants, 22
Greatest Show on Earth, The, 27
Greenfield, 24-5
Gucci, Aldo, 58, 59
Gucci, Guccio, 12, 57-8
Gucci, House of, 12, 55-62, 66-7
Gucci, Maurizio, 55-6, 58, 59, 60-1, 66
Gucci, Paolo, 59
Gucci, Patrizia, 56-7, 60, 61-2
Gucci, Rodolfo, 58
Guinness's, 83
Guinness, Arthur, 20
Guy Gannett Corporation, 181

Haji-Ionnou, Stelios, 110-1
Hamer, Dean, 28
Hanson, James, 61
Harris, Judith Rich, 36
Harvard Business School, 91-2
Harvey-Jones, Sir John, 171
Haughey, Charles, 69-70, 71
Hayes, Freda, 55, 75-8
Heffernan, Margaret, 70-1, 72-3
Hepburn, Audrey, 12
Hermés, 120
Hewlett, Bill, 16

Packard, David, 16, 17-8
Peron, Eva, 12
Polaroid, 19
Powerscreen, 42
Pratt, Maurice, 68
Pressman, Barney, 45-9
Pressman, Fred, 44, 46-9, 63-4, 65
Pressman, Gene, 64, 65-6
Pressman, Robert, 64
Prone, Terry, 118

Quinn, Feargal, 68

Raventós, Maria, 154-65
Repubblica, La, 109
Ryan, Dr Tony, 21-2
Ryanair, 21

Sacramento Bee, the, 84
Sara Lee Corporation, 177
Savage, Anton, 118
Savage, Tom, 118
Schafer, Jim, 181
Smyth, Philip, 165-6
St James's Gate, Dublin, 20, 83
Stanford University, 16
Sulloway, Frank, 23
Swanson, Gloria, 29

Thomas Crosbie Holdings, 148
Times, The, 10
Tour IT, 134
Troubleshooters, 171

UCD (University College Dublin), 134
UCLA, 25